Teaching Large Classes Well

Maryellen Gleason Weimer, *Editor*
Pennsylvania State University

NEW DIRECTIONS FOR TEACHING AND LEARNING
KENNETH E. EBLE, *Editor-in-Chief*
University of Utah, Salt Lake City

Number 32, Winter 1987

Paperback sourcebooks in
The Jossey-Bass Higher Education Series

Jossey-Bass Inc., Publishers
San Francisco • London

Maryellen Gleason Weimer (ed.).
Teaching Large Classes Well.
New Directions for Teaching and Learning, no. 32.
San Francisco: Jossey-Bass, Winter 1987.

New Directions for Teaching and Learning
Kenneth E. Eble, *Editor-in-Chief*

New Directions for Teaching and Learning is published quarterly
by Jossey-Bass Inc., Publishers, 433 California Street, San Francisco,
California, 94104. Application to mail at second-class postage rates
is pending at San Francisco, California, and at additional mailing
offices. POSTMASTER: Send address changes to *New Directions for
Teaching and Learning*, Jossey-Bass Inc., Publishers, 433 California
Street, San Francisco, California 94104.

Editorial correspondence should be sent to the Editor-in-Chief,
Kenneth E. Eble, Department of English, University of Utah,
Salt Lake City, Utah 84112.

Library of Congress Catalog Card Number LC 85-644763

International Standard Serial Number ISSN 0271-0633

International Standard Book Number ISBN 1-55542-934-3

Cover art by WILLI BAUM

Manufactured in the United States of America

Ordering Information

The paperback sourcebooks listed below are published quarterly and can be ordered either by subscription or single copy.

Subscriptions cost $48.00 per year for institutions, agencies, and libraries. Individuals can subscribe at the special rate of $36.00 per year *if payment is by personal check*. (Note that the full rate of $48.00 applies if payment is by institutional check, even if the subscription is designated for an individual.) Standing orders are accepted.

Single copies are available at $11.95 when payment accompanies order. (California, New Jersey, New York, and Washington, D.C., residents please include appropriate sales tax.) For billed orders, cost per copy is $11.95 plus postage and handling.

Substantial discounts are offered to organizations and individuals wishing to purchase bulk quantities of Jossey-Bass sourcebooks. Please inquire.

Please note that these prices are for the academic year 1987–88 and are subject to change without notice. Also, some titles may be out of print and therefore not available for sale.

To ensure correct and prompt delivery, all orders must give either the *name of an individual* or an *official purchase order number*. Please submit your order as follows:

Subscriptions: specify series and year subscription is to begin.
Single Copies: specify sourcebook code (such as, TL1) and first two words of title.

Mail orders for United States and Possessions, Latin America, Canada, Japan, Australia, and New Zealand to:
Jossey-Bass Inc., Publishers
433 California Street
San Francisco, California 94104

Mail orders for all other parts of the world to:
Jossey-Bass Limited
28 Banner Street
London EC1Y 8QE

New Directions for Teaching and Learning Series
Kenneth E. Eble, *Editor-in-Chief*

Contents

Editor's Notes

No one has offered hard evidence yet, but faculty at many institutions believe that the number and size of large course sections are on the rise. Large classes are so cost efficient that, as budget pressures increase in higher education, the temptation to increase course enrollments has great allure to administrators in higher education.

Generally, the use of large class sections does not receive accolades from students, parents, or faculty. For students, the environment of large classes tends to be impersonal and the opportunity for dialogue with the "great mind" teaching the course is almost nonexistent. For parents, it may seem unwise to spend a lot of money for an educational experience of dubious value. For faculty, teaching large sections is one of the most challenging of all academic experiences. As J. Richard Aronson observes in Chapter Three (this volume), "Your colleagues will treat you with great care, admiration, and respect. Why? Because they want you to keep teaching the course."

As with many of their teaching experiences, faculty are frequently ill-prepared to assume responsibility for large sections. Most college professors have not been trained to teach and tend to teach as they were taught. One problem that arises within this instructional environment is that errors tend to be magnified. As Robert P. Brooks observes in Chapter Four, "It is difficult to recover from a mistake made in front of one hundred students, not impossible, just difficult."

The assumption that these courses can be taught in much the same way other, smaller college courses are taught causes problems for faculty members in big classes—and for the department heads that put them there. Faculty under this assumption face a grim confrontation with reality: The large class is no place for a novice to learn how to teach.

Until now, though seasoned practitioners know of the problems and have implemented solutions, a practical compendium of advice on teaching and learning in large classes has not appeared in the literature. This volume is an attempt to remedy that omission. It is intended to provide faculty, who are teaching a large course for the first time, practical advice that will ease the transition from small, personal teaching environments to much less intimate ones. It is the sort of volume every department head should hand out along with teaching assignments for large sections, and pass on to colleagues who labor hard and conscientiously in these difficult instructional situations. It is also of interest and

1

value to those who regularly teach large classes. Teaching any number of students can always be improved, refreshed, and enlivened. This sourcebook can give an experienced instructor a new look at an old set of problems and offer new solutions and advice.

The chapters in this volume do not propose radical alterations in instructional methods and practices. They do propose alternatives. Too often, instructors in large courses resign themselves exclusively to lecturing. A number of authors in this sourcebook and the resources in the bibliography refute the necessity for this. They propose modifications and adaptations of tested instructional strategies. The trick is to change and adapt common teaching techniques that work well in small classes so they fit the constraints of the much larger classroom situation. That task is challenging but not impossible. In fact, if this volume has one aim, it is to make the task of teaching a large section manageable.

The authors in this volume assume class sizes of at least one hundred students. The decision to designate one hundred-student classes as large was made cognizant of the fact that some instructors teach classes of thirty students as if enrollment for the course were three hundred. The focus of this volume, however, is on classes in which the possibility of individual relationships between professor and student is precluded, in which not every student who wants to speak in class can be called on, and in which grading essay exams can take up every evening and weekend of the course.

This sourcebook contains a variety of material written from different perspectives. Knapper (Chapter One) and Wulff, Nyquist, and Abbott (in Chapter Two) look at large courses from a broad perspective, examining both the rationale and experience of teaching and learning in a large course. Aronson (Chapter Three) and Brooks (Chapter Four) write from the perspective of practitioners: "I do it and here's the best advice I can pass on to you." Frederick (Chapter Five) focuses on techniques: what instructors with large classes should do to discourage student passivity; Weaver and Cotrell (Chapter Six) on increasing effectiveness as lecturers; and Lowman (Chapter Seven) on constructively evaluating and grading large numbers of students. Finally, Murray (Chapter Eight) offers advice on gathering feedback from students, and Weimer and Kerns (Chapter Nine) identify sources of other potential solutions.

The volume does not try to condone large classes. Knapper's opening chapter relates the presence and likely continuation of large classes to current issues in higher education. One fact appears not to be arguable: Large classes have been part of the educational scene for many years and they will continue to be an educational experience for many students for the foreseeable future. To those students who will attend large classes, we have an obligation to do something more than debate the propriety of various class sizes. To the faculty teaching large classes, learning to teach them well is a fundamental professional obligation.

Maryellen Gleason Weimer
Editor

Maryellen Gleason Weimer is head of the Instructional Development Program at the Pennsylvania State University. She edits a monthly newsletter for faculty, The Teaching Professor.

Of great importance in large class instruction is the need to ensure that students learn how to learn so that they may take from the course the knowledge, skills, and attitudes that can serve them well the rest of their lives.

Large Classes and Learning

Christopher Knapper

The late 1980s are a time of considerable frustration for many university faculty—especially those of us who take teaching seriously and worry about the quality of learning we are imparting to our students. In the United States, Canada, Western Europe, and beyond, higher education institutions have seen their budgets cut, their values challenged, and their instructional practices called into question. In 1986, the National Governors' Association issued a report saying that: "Many colleges and universities do not have a systematic way to demonstrate whether student learning is taking place. Rather, learning—and especially developing abilities to utilize knowledge—is assumed to take place as long as students take courses, accumulate hours, and progress 'satisfactorily' towards a degree" (Fiske, 1987, p. 1). The governors challenged higher education institutions to show they merit continued investment of public funds.

Calls by politicians for universities to demonstrate value added benefits of higher education, though probably simplistic, reflect the mood of the times. Meanwhile, faculty must bear the burden of inexorably increasing workloads—manifested almost universally in increasing faculty-student ratios and ever-larger classes.

Higher Education and the Goals of Learning

Given this context, it is not surprising that a book on teaching large classes would find a ready audience among a beleaguered professo-

M. G. Weimer (ed.). *Teaching Large Classes Well.*
New Directions for Teaching and Learning, no. 32. San Francisco: Jossey-Bass, Winter 1987.

riate, eager to find some pragmatic answers to the problems of dealing effectively with packed classrooms. Yet at the risk of antagonizing readers who admit to being already hard-pressed, we must postpone a discussion of remedies and begin by tackling some fundamental issues about the purpose of a university education, the type of learning we wish to encourage, and how such learning objectives might be facilitated by our methods of teaching, including the way we teach large classes. In other words, before we decide the way we teach, let us decide why we teach and what we hope our students will learn as a result.

The past three years have seen a spate of reports about the quality of education in the United States, issued by organizations such as the National Institute of Education, the National Endowment for the Humanities, the Association of American Colleges, and the Carnegie Foundation for the Advancement of Education. Ernest Boyer, in his 1986 report for the Carnegie Foundation, offers a number of criticisms of contemporary higher education institutions (Carnegie Foundation . . . , 1986). He raises issues of confusion over academic goals, problems of faculty training and renewal (especially related to teaching), the quality of teaching and student assessment, cross purposes of campus academic and social life, difficulties in measuring the quality and outcomes of higher education, and failure to forge strong links between the academic environment and the outside world.

Implicit in these criticisms is a set of goals for university education. Although some of the reports mentioned above have sparked controversy in the academic community, most of the underlying assumptions about the type of learning ideally produced in a university would, we suspect, be widely accepted by faculty. To summarize themes that run through a number of the commentaries, the ideal products of our universities should be:
- Creative, independent problem-solvers
- Capable of learning from life and throughout life
- Able to integrate insights from different fields and disciplines
- Able to communicate effectively, both orally and in writing
- Skilled at dealing with people and able to work individually and with groups
- Sensitive to ethical and moral issues in life and work situations.

Cross (1987) has even tried to spell out the characteristics of good teachers that might foster such aims. They include encouraging contacts with students, stressing active learning, having students reflect on their learning and try to relate it to their daily lives, providing students with prompt feedback on their performance, and respecting diverse talents and ways of learning.

The notion that a primary goal of higher education is to produce independent, self-directed, lifelong learners is, of course, far from new.

Cardinal Newman (1973[1852]) articulated similar educational aims over a hundred years ago, and the basic notion can be traced back much further. More recently, critics of education, including Edgar Faure (in his work for UNESCO) and members of the Club of Rome, have called for close scrutiny of contemporary educational practices and questioned our ability to prepare students adequately for an increasingly complex world that is undergoing unprecedented social and technological change (Botkin, Elmandjra, and Malitza, 1979; Faure, 1972).

Building on the work of these theorists, Knapper and Cropley (1985) have argued the need for universities to move away from an emphasis on teaching content and toward helping students acquire skills to "learn how to learn." They argue that much knowledge, especially in the technical fields, becomes rapidly outdated and may bear little relationship to needed skills and tasks performed in real-life situations. Hence, universities should concentrate on equipping students with more problem-solving skills, recognizing that people continue to learn almost daily throughout their lives and mostly in situations where they cannot call upon formal educational institutions to help them.

Learning Goals and Large Classes

This raises an important academic policy question of whether such learning goals are easily achievable in large classes, which may contain one hundred, three hundred, or even more than five hundred students. Classes of this size put severe restrictions on the possibility for interaction between instructor and students and presumably make it difficult to achieve the type of class spirit and sense of community that were important features of university education when institutions and class sizes were much smaller. Many of the critics of contemporary education mentioned above have linked their comments about teaching and learning methods to concerns about the quality of student life in universities. They express concern that the impersonality and lack of academic community may be encouraged by large classes. Such classes can inhibit the cross-fertilization of ideas and integration of knowledge from different disciplines that many academics espouse as an important goal of higher education.

Organizational and Administrative Issues

Although this sourcebook is based on the premise that teaching large classes is going to continue, important decisions have to be made about when large class sections are appropriate and when they are unacceptable. It may appear that such matters are outside the control of the individual faculty member; however, instructors have a role in depart-

mental and institutional policy making and sit on curriculum commit-
tees that often decide matters of course format and class size as well as
choice of instructor. In many cases the decision to teach large numbers of
students at one time may be a necessary evil brought about by budgetary
constraints, lack of available classrooms, or shortage of qualified personnel. In such circumstances it is important to make decisions at the
institutional and departmental levels that will maximize the chances of
success. For example, while a large class format may be unavoidable, this
does not necessarily imply that all teaching must take place in the live
classroom setting with all students present. The class could conceivably
meet as a whole just once a week, with alternative instructional strategies,
for example, computer-based instruction, student syndicates, and independent learning methods such as Keller's (1974) Personalized System of
Instruction (PSI) used as a supplement.

Another departmental decision concerns the choice of instructor.
It is intuitively obvious and has been shown empirically by the results of
teaching evaluations that not all instructors enjoy or succeed in teaching
large groups of students, and it is common sense to ensure that such
classes are handled by faculty who flourish in this setting. Relevant characteristics include ability to communicate clearly to a large audience
(which involves appropriate use of both voice and gestures—in other
words, capacity to perform in an almost theatrical sense) as well as organizational skills to deal with logistical problems. The latter concern not
only dealing with students directly but also making most effective use of
teaching assistants who generally handle a good deal of the instructional
burden in large classes.

To recapitulate, while most of this sourcebook is concerned with
the problem of the individual instructor who has already been assigned a
large class to teach, instructors also have an input into the administrative
issues of how classes are to be taught and organized as well as who will
teach them—and these academic responsibilities must be taken seriously
if effective learning is to be achieved.

Specifying Course Objectives

Another important decision that should be made well before
embarking on teaching a class (large or small) is a clarification of course
objectives. Is the intention to cover content, that is, concentrate upon
factual information and so-called basic concepts in the subject area? Is
the aim to teach skills, for example, analytical or problem-solving skills?
Or is the main goal to increase students' motivation or change attitudes?

A common use of large classes is in introductory courses that provide students with their first exposure to a discipline. Here the course
content and orientation is best decided not by the individual instructor

in charge of the course but by the department as a whole. Even when this is done conscientiously by a departmental curriculum committee, frequently history and precedent (reflected, for example, in the standard textbooks for the discipline) play a major role in determining course content and emphasis—as opposed to a careful scrutiny of desired outcomes for the course in terms of appropriate student knowledge, skills, and attitudes.

If the course is intended primarily as an introduction to further work in the discipline it makes sense to ask instructors of upper-level courses what type of knowledge and skills are required of incoming students. When this is done systematically through a detailed curriculum-planning process the results often have surprising implications for prerequisites courses. For example, a review of the curriculum in Chemical Engineering at the University of Queensland, (Newell, Lee, and Leung, 1985) resulted in major changes to course content and teaching methods. While large class lectures were retained, their number was substantially reduced, and they were used not to transmit content, but instead to discuss or demonstrate a few basic, important ideas in the field. Factual material was prepared in a set of written course notes that were handed to students for use in independent study. Deciding on appropriate course goals and learning outcomes is important in any discipline but is especially vital in professional education where facts are usually subservient to problem-solving skills. This may be why some of the most radical curriculum innovations have been made in fields such as medicine and engineering—despite the fact that a great deal of teaching for these professions also remains traditional.

Teaching Methods

If the ultimate goals of higher education in a discipline are not attended to, the result may be classes that are merely rituals that students attend as passively empty vessels to be filled with the accumulated (and often idiosyncratic) wisdom of the professor. Even assuming that acquisition of the basic facts of the discipline is a primary aim of the course, it is doubtful whether the traditional lecture method is the best means of accomplishing this end. For example, Bligh's (1972) review of research on the lecture method compared to other instructional approaches shows that it is not especially effective, even for conveying content—largely because a good deal of the content presented by the instructor is not attended to by students and what is attended to may be distorted on its path from the lecturer's notes to the students'. An interesting exercise for instructors of large classes who wish to monitor students' perception of lecture content is to take a sample of notebooks and compare them with each other and with the instructor's own notes.

Citing these limitations of the lecture method for conveying factual information, some educational theorists have recommended using large classes as motivational devices to stimulate interest in a subject or demonstrate concepts, while leaving transmission of basic information to other instructional media such as textbooks or specially written modules. For example, this is the approach advocated by Keller (1974) in his Personalized System of Instruction (PSI), which has been used successfully in many thousands of courses in North American colleges and universities. Whether or not some innovative approach of this type is used, if the basic aim of a course is to convey facts, the instructor in charge of a large class might consider strategies for disseminating information by other means than lecturing (perhaps handing out the lecture notes) and use class time to convey some of the excitement of the discipline. Later chapters describe a number of techniques for doing this.

Assessing Student Learning

When scrutinizing the teaching methods in large classes it is important to consider the way in which student learning is assessed and graded—a vital aspect of instruction. We often equate teaching with the instructor's classroom performance, but in fact this is only one aspect of the teaching/learning process. For the student, the learning situation also involves a great deal of work outside the classroom and the opportunity to get advice from teaching assistants, fellow students, or the professor in charge of the course. More important, a good deal of research on student learning indicates that major motivating forces for study are the assignments and examinations rather than what is said in lectures. Hence, preparation for teaching a large class must take into account not only the instructional methods but also how student learning is to be assessed, bearing in mind, of course, that the evaluation methods should be consistent with instructional goals.

This presents a major problem when student numbers are very large. For example, the objectives for the course may emphasize changing attitudes toward the discipline or ability to grasp complex theories, yet assessment may be based primarily on multiple-choice tests that are more suited to measuring recall of factual information. If the goals stress acquisition of complex skills, then assessment should test application of these skills in situations that are as realistic as possible. Unfortunately this may be hard to achieve, logistically, when a class contains hundreds of students. Yet another problem of assessment in large classes is the difficult of providing detailed and rapid feedback on students' work. It may not be easy to set regular assignments throughout the term. And, even is this is done, grading becomes an immense task—especially to go beyond the simple indication of a grade to include individual comments. At the same time, such feedback is highly desirable if students are to learn from the assessment exercise and do better on subsequent tasks. Information from the professor on learning progress is also important for sustaining motivation.

Although it is difficult to provide regular and meaningful assessment when class numbers are large, some shortcuts are possible. These include use of "assignment attachments" (specially prepared forms showing common errors that markers can follow and supplement by short written comments) or use of class time to give feedback on a test or assignment to the group as a whole.

Learning to Learn

A related challenge to instructors of large classes is how to go beyond teaching content to help students master skills of effective learning that are often mistakenly taken for granted. For example, most faculty want their students to do more than simply regurgitate information presented in lectures (what Marton and Saljo, 1976, have referred to as "surface" learning). Indeed, most teachers see their courses as a preparation for further study in the field—something that students will build upon long after they leave the class.

As teachers what help do we give students to acquire these analysis skills, to make decisions on the basis of the best available information, and to solve both familiar and unanticipated problems? When we set student assignments, how much attention do we give to the way the task is to be approached—ranging from library research techniques to presentation of written reports? These often neglected aspects of instruction are essential if we are to foster independent lifelong learning, and are just as important in large introductory courses as they are in small upper-level situations. It might be argued that the first- and second-year classes that frequently attract very large enrollments are more crucial for teaching independent learning and communications skills, simply because they set the tone for a student's whole academic career. Once again the objection can be raised that it is much more difficult to teach such skills effectively when student numbers are large. The matter is further complicated by the fact that students vary considerably in their learning styles and orientations, and a uniform, lock-step approach to teaching (which the lecture method almost inevitably implies) cannot accommodate such individual differences.

The Role of Teaching Assistants

Some solutions are possible. For example, in many cases, large courses have smaller seminars or tutorials run by teaching assistants. These provide a marvelous opportunity for working with students in smaller groups and tackling problems that would be impractical to address in the large class. Yet very often this chance is wasted by teaching assistants (TAs) who use the time to give mini-lectures on topics that have already been covered. One reason for this situation is that teaching assistants often receive little, if any, training and hence lack the skills necessary to run an effective discussion group, give individual help and advice, and devise appropriate tutorial tasks that might foster student learning in keeping with the overall course goals.

At the University of Waterloo several years ago, the introductory course in English composition, which involved classes of several hundred students, was completely reorganized to achieve more effective mastery of writing skills. Lectures to the whole class were cut down from three hours a week to one and were revamped to place more emphasis on capturing students' imagination, while providing feedback on students' writing was done in tutorials comprised of relatively small groups of about fifteen students each. The tutors were carefully trained by the course instructor in running the sessions to ensure full and productive discussion and were trained in marking assignments to yield reliable grades and provide helpful student feedback. The instructor designed the tutorials, conducted the training sessions, and met weekly with TAs to monitor progress, sort out problems, and so on. A careful plan for assessing the effectiveness of tutorials included self-assessment by TAs, appraisals by students, and reports on visits to the sessions by both the instructor and a consultant from the instructional development office. This process did not reduce the professor's commitment of time to the course, but instead involved a restructuring of his duties, with fewer hours spent in front of the large class and more time devoted to organizational matters and liaison with TAs. One result was a marked improvement in instructional effectiveness, judged by student satisfaction and enhanced writing skills.

This example is not cited as a universal solution for teaching large classes. (Among other things, TA support may not be available in some circumstances.) Instead, it is meant to show that improving teaching effectiveness for large groups of students does not necessarily involve changing classroom techniques, but may require more fundamental organizational matters. Before leaving the issue of student learning skills and the importance of explicitly teaching them, it is worth mentioning that the need becomes especially crucial with nontraditional students, such as minority groups and mature students, who may lack certain entry skills and require special assistance and support.

Research on Student Learning

One obstacle to teaching large classes in a way that will encourage independent learning and more sophisticated levels of understanding is that few faculty have ever received formal training in pedagogy and, perhaps most important, many appear to have forgotten how students learn. Recent research on the way that university students tackle learning tasks suggest two contrasting approaches to studying that Marton and Saljo (1976) have referred to as "deep" and "surface." This research further indicates that the way learning takes place is not solely through innate ability, but is very much influenced by the type of teaching students are exposed to.

For example, Watkins (1983) has shown that inappropriate instruction and assessment methods can produce students who become less sophisticated learners over the course of a three-year undergraduate degree program. On a more positive note, Ramsden and Entwistle (1981) identified teaching practices that improved deep-level learning for undergraduate students enrolled in a British university. Attributes of effective teaching identified by the researchers included a reasonable workload, opportunities for students to interact with faculty, and flexibility in approaches to assessment. While all this is perhaps more difficult to achieve in large classes, ignoring this research evidence has demonstrable consequences for the quality of learning.

Barriers to Change

One complicating factor is that unfortunately many students enter higher education with attitudes that favor traditional didactic teaching—thus encouraging student passivity and adoption of surface learning techniques simply because they are easier. On the other hand, students seek relevance and involvement and we argue that failure to equip them with appropriate independent lifelong learning skills will have unfortunate consequences for both students and the institution in the long term. Recall, too, that our universities will depend on these graduates for political and financial support in the future.

Another barrier to organizational change in the structuring of large classes are the institutional traditions that often equate learning with classes that meet three or four hours a week for thirteen weeks a semester. This view is reinforced by the perceptions of outside credentialing bodies (such as professional associations in medicine and engineering) that exert indirect influence on the curriculum. In reality, there is often a good deal more freedom in the organization of courses, including such matters as the number of formal lectures, than many faculty assume. And when changes prove to be successful, as in the above examples, this can often have a ripple effect throughout the institution.

Conclusions

Given that large classes are a fact of life in most institutions, the issue is how we can best plan and use them to fulfill worthwhile learning objectives. The above discussion suggests a series of questions that faculty might ask themselves before beginning to organize a course that will involve scores or hundreds of students.

1. What are the overall objectives of the course and the expected outcomes, and how do they relate to general departmental and institutional goals? Do the objectives emphasize acquisition of facts, understanding of theoretical constructs, mastery of intellectual skills, or assimilation of values or attitudes?

2. How are these objectives to be assessed in the course, allowing for logistical constraints of manpower and funds, and bearing in mind the need to tailor assessment methods to the type of learning expected and the desirability of providing students with feedback that they can use as a basis for improvement?

3. What will be the general format of the course, especially the balance between large lecture settings and other learning arrangements, such as smaller tutorial groups, independent learning, peer study groups, and so on? In particular, how will different learning styles be accommodated?

4. What specific teaching approaches and techniques (not restricted to didactic lectures) can be used to foster desired learning objectives, both in the large classroom setting and beyond? In the case of lectures, how much material can be covered, given the evidence about limitations on student attention span and retention of orally presented material?

5. If teaching assistants are employed, to what extent are they aware of the learning objectives for the course, how will they be trained for teaching, assessment, and advisory roles, and what procedures are in place to allow frequent liaison between TAs and the instructor in charge of the course?

6. What strategies will be employed to stimulate self-directed learning or learning-to-learn techniques that students can apply outside the classroom? And how much of this can be achieved in the large class setting as opposed to smaller tutorial groups or even outside the classroom?

7. Finally, what steps will be taken to evaluate course effectiveness in relation to the learning objectives? Possibilities include use of student evaluations, peer assessment of both classroom activities and course materials, retrospective comments by former students, and indication of the extent to which students are adequately prepared for subsequent courses in the discipline.

With these questions as a blueprint for planning, remaining chapters examine some tangible ways in which learning in large classes can be made more effective.

References

Bligh, D. A. *What's the Use of Lectures?* Harmondsworth, England: Penguin, 1972.

Botkin, J. W., Elmandjra, M., and Malitza, M. *No Limits to Learning.* Elmsford, N. Y.: Pergamon Press, 1979.

Carnegie Foundation for the Advancement of Education. *College: The Undergraduate Experience.* New York: Carnegie Foundation, 1986.

Cross, K. P. "The Teacher as a Classroom Researcher." Paper presented at the annual meeting of the American Association for Higher Education, Chicago, March 1987.

Faure, E., Merrera, F., Kaddoura, A., Lepes, H., Petrovsky, A., Rahnema, M., and Ward, F. C. *Learning to Be: The World of Education Today and Tommorow.* Paris and London: UNESCO and Harrap, 1972.

Fiske, E. B. "Colleges Prodded to Prove Worth." *New York Times,* January 18, 1987, pp. 1, 12.

Keller, F. S. *PSI: The Keller Plan Handbook.* Menlo Park, Calif.: Benjamin-Cummings, 1974.

Knapper, C. K., and Cropley, A. J. *Lifelong Learning and Higher Education.* London: Croom, Helm, 1985.

Marton, F., and Saljo, R. "On Qualitative Differences in Learning II: Outcome as a Function of Learner's Conception of Task." *British Journal of Educational Psychology,* 1976, *46,* 115–117.

Newell, R. B., Lee, P. L., and Leung, L. S. "A Resource-Based Approach to ChE Education." *Chemical Engineering Education,* Winter 1985, 36–50.

Newman, J. H. *The Idea of a University.* Westminster, Md.: Christian Classics, 1973. (Originally published 1852.)

Ramsden, P., and Entwistle, N. J. "Effects of Academic Departments on Students' Approaches to Studying." *British Journal of Educational Psychology,* 1981, *51,* 368–383.

Watkins, D. "Assessing Tertiary Study Processes." *Human Learning,* 1983, *2,* 29–37.

Christopher Knapper is director of Teaching Resources and Continuing Education and professor of environmental studies at the University of Waterloo. He has published numerous books and articles on the evaluation and improvement of university teaching, most recently Lifelong Learning and Higher Education, *coauthored with Arthur Cropley (1985).*

The crucial variable seems to be not so much the size as the effectiveness of the instructor in the class.

Students' Perceptions of Large Classes

Donald H. Wulff, Jody D. Nyquist, Robert D. Abbott

For many years, researchers have studied the effects of class size on teaching effectiveness and student learning. Although such research has yielded conflicting results and few answers, it has reinforced the idea that large-class instruction is a complicated process that is affected by numerous instructional dimensions. Sorting out those dimensions and understanding their complex interactions is just beginning. This volume helps instructors focus on the dimensions that can make a difference in the quality of learning and teaching in large classes. An important part of understanding these dimensions resides in a consideration of the students' perspectives. This chapter summarizes some major dimensions of students' perceptions of instruction in large classes.

A Conception of Large-Class Instruction

The general belief has been that increased class size dictates a lower quality of instruction and that as classes get larger, students' learning and degree of satisfaction decrease. Experience suggests that size is, indeed, a factor that influences the way classes are taught. We do not

M. G. Weimer (ed.). *Teaching Large Classes Well.*
New Directions for Teaching and Learning, no. 32. San Francisco: Jossey-Bass, Winter 1987.

believe, however, that size is the major determinant of the success of a class. In fact, large classes can, in many respects, be just as effective as small classes (Feldman, 1984; Marsh, Overall, Kesler, 1979; Williams, Cook, Quinn, and Jensen, 1985). On our campus, large-class instructors' student ratings rival the ratings for the best small-class instructors. In addition, students have told us that the quality of instruction, not size determines how successful classes will be. Therefore, a discussion of students' perceptions of instruction in large classes begins with a brief explanation of three basic assumptions about teaching large classes.

First, we believe that teaching is a complex process. Whether we are working in large classes or small classes, the teaching-learning process produces complex interactions among instructor, students, content, and context—creating a variety of interacting dimensions. Large classes increase the potential for complex interactions as well as constraints on content and physical space. Meeting the needs of individual students while still accomplishing important instructional goals becomes increasingly complex. This complexity suggests that it is important for instructors of large classes to understand the interacting dimensions in the teaching-learning process. One aspect of this understanding depends on identifying how students view and prioritize various instructional dimensions.

A second major assumption is that effective teaching is a process of adaptation or adjustment of these multiple dimensions. Because teaching is a dynamic process, the need for focusing on particular variables can change readily from one context to another; and there are few clear-cut guidelines for success. Effective teachers, however, make decisions that help them to balance important instructional dimensions. Although the dimensions are the same whether a class is large or small, the ways they are adjusted to account for the differences in class size may differ significantly. For instance, although rapport is an important dimension in both large and small classes, the importance accorded rapport and the way it is developed may be influenced by the number of students in the class. To adjust their teaching, instructors need information not only about the important dimensions but also about how those dimensions can be balanced for the benefit of all. Knowing how students interpret and value major instructional dimensions enables an instructor to make informed decisions to enhance the teaching-learning process.

Our third assumption is that students create their own interpretation about a particular instructional context. Very often we find that the mental models students use to interpret what's happening in their classes are very different from those assumed by the instructors or trained observers in the classroom. More than once, we have discovered inconsistencies between our observations of a class and what students thought was happening in the class. Information about the factors that influence the way students experience instruction can be identified through their self-reports. Knowing how students perceive instruction can assist the instructor who is selecting from a variety of alternative instructional approaches.

These assumptions about instruction suggest why research focusing on global variables such as class size have produced conflicting results. Perhaps it is time, then, to look beyond the size variable to the specific instructional dimensions that interact within the context of various-sizes classes. We have begun to examine these interactions by assessing students' perceptions of important instructional dimensions in the large class and by having students provide insights about adapting such dimensions to provide the most productive teaching-learning experiences.

Gathering Students' Perceptions of Teaching in Large Classes

To gather information on students' perceptions of instructional dimensions in large classes, we have, for three years, systematically collected data, primarily through standardized questionnaires administered in lower-division large classes. Questionnaires have provided opportunities for students to select and describe the best and worst classes they have ever taken. After identifying these, students rated the classes on standardized ratings forms and generated their own categories of instructional dimensions by responding to open-ended questions. Students' responses to open-ended questions about large-class instruction have been systematically categorized to help us understand what assists and what hinders learning in large classes and what improvements students would suggest. After administering variations of the questionnaires to over eight hundred students at the University of Washington, we have begun to understand how students perceive large classes that, on this campus, are predominantly offered at the freshman and sophomore levels. Although their perceptions are varied and sometimes conflicting, students do reinforce the importance of focusing on the dimensions of effective teaching rather than the number of students in the large class. Some students felt that the quality of large classes "depends less on size than quality of instruction."

Students' Overall Perceptions of the Large-Class Context

Although we heard about students' distaste for large classes, we had little systematic data to clarify how students think about large classes at the university level. We were unsure, for instance, how students define the word *large* when they use it in reference to large classes. Although much of the research has focused on students' ratings of classes, most definitions of the term *large class* have arbitrarily been established from the perspective of researchers, faculty, or administrators. In addition, research on large classes and remarks from students provided no clear indication whether students, in fact, preferred classes of a certain size. Since we felt that insights on these issues were essential to understanding students' perceptions of large classes, we asked students two questions: (1) At what point do classes become large? and (2) Which class size do you prefer for freshman- and sophomore-level classes?

Responses provided no clear evidence that students defined large classes in one way or that they all preferred classes of a specific size. Of the over 800 students who responded to the question asking them to identify the point at which a class becomes large, 2 percent perceived that this happens when enrollment reaches 25; 16 percent when enrollment reaches 50; and 22 percent when enrollment reaches 75. The largest percentage of students in any one category (24 percent) reported that classes become large when they reach an enrollment of 100 students. Another 13 percent indicated that they perceived classes to be large at 150 students, while 24 percent indicated that an enrollment of 200 or above meant a large class. A majority of the students (58 percent), then, reported that classes become large somewhere between 75 and 150 students.

Of the 327 students who were asked what class size they preferred for lower division courses, only 5 percent of the respondents preferred classes enrolling fewer than 25 students. The largest percentage of students in any one category (23 percent) preferred classes of 25–50 students. An additional 14 percent preferred classes of 50–75 students, while another 17 percent of the respondents preferred class sizes of 75–100 students. Another 18 percent of the students preferred classes with enrollments of 200 or more. Rather surprisingly, then, 41 percent of the students actually preferred classes with enrollments of 100 students or more, an enrollment size which many of them defined as "large."

Additional insight was gained when we asked students to rate the quality of the best large and best small class they had ever taken at this university on the dimension of "course as a whole." Results showed no significant difference in students' ratings of their best large and their best small classes.

These data suggest that some of the myths about large classes need to be qualified. Although some students clearly preferred small classes, many students liked, and even preferred, what they defined as large classes. Whereas a number of students recommended elimination of large classes as a way to improve instruction, suggesting that the larger size hinders their learning, many others reported that they liked large classes. Additional insights about students' conflicting perceptions were obtained by studying their responses to open-ended questions about what assisted them or hindered their learning in large classes.

Students' Positive Comments. Categorization of positive comments about what assisted students in learning in the large class context produced four factors that were a direct result of the increased student enrollment.

Other Students. The most frequently cited contextual factor was other students. In response to what assists them in learning in large classes, students responded that next to professors the most important ingredient was the presence of lots of other students—"more people to get to know, to study with, to talk to, to have fun with, to compare notes with."

Low-Pressure Element. A second factor was the low-pressure element in the large class. A number of students, for instance, felt they were assisted in their learning by the relaxed, low-pressure, anonymous context for learning. Specifically, students suggested that there was "not as much pressure during class time" or that there was a "sense of security" so that they were "not nervous." Others appreciated the "anonymous-type feeling," "not being singled out," or being able to "hide" or lose themselves in the crowd so they "don't have to come, answer, or interact."

Sense of Independence. A third source of positive reaction to large classes arose from the sense of independence created by the context. Students indicated that the large class gives them a "feeling of independence" so that learning was assisted by "reliance of self" and having "to study and learn" themselves.

Variety of Attendance Options. Finally, for some students the large-class context provided a variety of attendance options that, in their perceptions, were positive because they could "skip without notice," "sleep," and "show up anytime."

Students' Negative Comments. Although some students indicated there were certain dimensions of large classes they liked, others were very clear about some of the contextual problems that resulted from the large-class atmosphere.

Lessened Individual Responsibility. The most frequently mentioned problem for these students was that the large class provided an atmosphere in which there was lessened individual responsibility. Students who responded in this way saw the passive context as hindering their learning: "It is easier to do anything you want, sleep, not attend, or lose attention."

Impersonal Nature. The second major hindrance on which students focused was the impersonal nature of the large class context. Students who focused on this weakness suggested that the large-class atmosphere was one of anonymity in which they felt lost or out of place, stating that there are "so many people, no one knows I'm here" or "troubled students fall by the wayside." These factors, according to the students, led to decreased motivation.

Noise and Distractions. A third major hindrance was noise and distractions. Students suggested that their learning was hindered by the continuous talking and comings and goings of other students—"rude people who come late," "leave early," or "sit and talk to their buddies."

Concerns of inadequate physical space and equipment typically focused on overcrowding, lack of seats, or distance from professors and visual aids—"small desk space," "overcrowding in stuffy environment," or inability "to hear professor or see the screen." The students were most concerned when there were difficulties with microphones or when ways to project written materials were unavailable or projected images were difficult to see.

Students' Perceptions of Content and Amount Learned

In addition to obtaining some sense of students' perceptions of the large-class context, we also compiled insights about more specific instructional dimensions of curriculum. Those insights were obtained both by comparing students' ratings of their best large and small classes regarding relevance and usefulness of course content and amount learned and by analyzing students' responses to open-ended questions. Although curriculum was not a primary factor in assisting or hindering students' learning, a number of students considered course content as a factor in distinguishing large classes from small classes.

Content. Students' ratings of the relevance and usefulness of course content in their best large class was not significantly different from that of their best small class. Apparently the size of the class did not systematically affect the way these students perceived the usefulness and relevance of course content.

When asked in open-ended questions what assisted them in learning in large classes, many students mentioned the breadth of coverage of content. Their general sense was that large classes were appropriate for presenting basic or general information. For instance, many students perceived that in large classes "the content is less detailed," "more general," "broader," and "usually good for any person to learn." Additionally, some suggested that such a presentation of content provides the opportunity "to get more ideas" as it is "diverse enough for all to relate to." A few respondents suggested that the content in large classes is "good introductory material" that is inherently interesting and "easy to learn."

Although some students felt that the large-class context was a place to provide basic content or general introduction to a discipline, many others felt that content suffered unnecessarily in large classes. Some felt that because of the breadth of coverage, too much information was covered too quickly. Typically, students who mentioned content as a hindering factor in large classes suggested that the content was too general and, consequently, boring.

Amount Learned. Although the students did not specifically refer to the amount learned in their responses to open-ended questions, on the questionnaire they did rate their satisfaction with their best large class and their best small class as to amount learned in the course. Again, a comparison of the ratings indicated that students did not rate their best large classes significantly different from their best small classes in this respect.

Students' Perceptions of Specific Instructional Dimensions

Instructor Dimensions. If we operate on the assumption that large classes can, on many instructional dimensions, be just as effective as small classes, we recognize the importance of the role of instructors in large classes. When students rated instructor's effectiveness in teaching, they gave significantly higher ratings to the instructors in the best large classes. When asked what assisted them in learning in large classes, they most frequently responded with comments about the professor. These findings reinforce the notion that according to students, the instructor plays an important role in the success of large classes.

From the student perspective, instructors could either help or hinder learning. In their open-ended comments students were very clear about their expectations for instructors. Although many students suggested the importance of "good" or "excellent" professors, some students were specific enough to identify four professor characteristics that were important to them.

Instructor Competency. Students want large-class professors who are knowledgeable. They perceive that the more "experienced" or "qualified" professors can really supply the necessary ingredients for successful large-class instruction.

Instructor Concern for Students. According to students, professors can assist learning if they are "caring, friendly, personable, interested in students and their points of view," or able to "use humor to relate to students." On the other hand, learning can be hindered if the "professor doesn't care," "is more interested in research," "shows lack of interest in whether students learn," and, consequently, "assumes understanding" or "is unaware of student confusion." The instructor's interest in whether students learned was one dimension in which students' best small classes were significantly better than their best large classes. This perception may be related to students' concern with the lack of availability of professors and teaching assistants in the large classes. In response to the question about what hinders their learning in large classes, some students indicated that there is "no help when it is needed" because of "unavailability of the instructor or the TA."

Instructor Energy Level. A third major instructor characteristic that enhanced learning was instructor energy level: a professor who is "enthusiastic" or "dynamic."

Instructor Speaking Ability. Students perceived that good speakers were good lecturers who could "keep attention," "maintain interest," and decrease "boredom." Many students suggested that "boring professors" and "boring lectures" were major factors that hindered their learning. Other important aspects that students mentioned were related to the speaker's clarity, rate of speech, inflection, and volume. Many students complained that professors were unclear, presented material too quickly, spoke in monotones, and could not always be heard. Students preferred professors who "avoid monotone," and were "easy to understand and listen to."

Although students focused heavily on professors in response to what assists them in learning, some students also suggested that teaching assistants (TAs) assisted or hindered their learning in large classes. Students endorsed the use of lots of "helpful and well-informed TAs" who were available at a variety of times. Students also perceived, however, that many of the TAs were "poor," "ineffective," and, in some cases, "incompetent." To be helpful, according to the students, TAs needed to be willing and not "too busy to help individual students." To be well-informed, TAs needed to be knowledgeable about the course content and, particularly if they were serving in a lab or a quiz section of a large class, they needed to attend lectures. Students indicated certain elements of quiz sections that enhanced learning, for example, "effective quiz sections," "smaller, more personal quiz sections," "more quiz sections with choices of teaching assistants," "interesting, informative quiz sections," "quiz sections twice a week," "quiz sections that give a different perspective, and well-taught quiz sections." Students were concerned, however, about the inconsistencies that arose from lack of communication between the large class and the quiz sections or labs and from inequities in the approaches taken by TAs in different quiz sections of the same large class. The role of the TA as instructor opens another enormously complicated dimension of the large class, especially when TAs are inadequately prepared for their assigned tasks. Our own attempt to address issues regarding the TA as instructor have been discipline and course specific (Nyquist and Wulff, 1987).

Another professors and TAs make many personal contributions, other instructional elements can improve the quality of large-class instruction. The following section focuses on some of the other instructional dimensions identified by students.

Interaction Between Students and Instructor. The greatest discrepancy between students' ratings of their best large classes and their best small classes was in interaction. Students rated their best small classes significantly better than their best large classes on the dimensions of instructor-student interaction. Also, when students were asked what hinders them in their large classes, by far the most frequent response was the lack of interaction between instructor and students. Students described hindrances to learning due to an "impersonal relationship" in which they had little "contact with the professor" or couldn't "talk to the professor when they misunderstand." A second major concern was the lack of opportunity to ask questions. Students perceived that frequently in their large classes there was "no opportunity for questions," or it was "harder to ask questions," sometimes because of "the professors' unwillingness to answer questions" or because of students' "fear of feeling stupid." This perception was especially important because the opportunity to ask questions served not only as a way to clarify misunderstandings but also as a way to take advantage of the variety of perspectives in the large class. As students expressed it, it is helpful to hear "input from other students," "questions by others to help clarify," or "the variety of questions asked by students." An essential interactional characteristic that assisted learning in the large class, when it occurred, was some type of discussion component. Students indicated that "audience reaction," "class discussion," and "input from a variety of backgrounds" contributed to their learning in the large class. Others indicated that their learning was hindered by the "dispension of discussion responsibilities."

Organization. Instructor organization and clarity were dimensions on which instructors in large classes could be just as successful as instructors in small classes. Students rated their best large class significantly higher than their best small class on the dimension of instructor organization and clarity. In response to open-ended questions, students typically mentioned the importance of "organization of the instructor," "clear, organized lectures," or "clarity of expectations." Students suggested that they were assisted in their learning when the instructor provided an overview of expectations at the beginning of each class, outlined major points on the overhead projector, presented an organized lecture, and repeated important statements to make sure they were clear. For some students, it was helpful when the instructor followed a familiar organizational format such as that presented in the text or a course syllabus.

Examples and Illustrations. Another area in which students rated their satisfaction in their best large class as significantly higher than in their best small class was instructor's use of examples and illustrations. Although some students simply suggested that the use of examples was helpful, others were more specific in suggesting that learning is assisted by professors' "giving examples of theory," "using a large number of examples pertaining to the material," and "using examples everyone can relate to." Demonstrations and analogies were mentioned as two specific kinds of examples that were particularly useful. Examples with humor were also mentioned as a way to make the content in the large class more engaging.

Instructional Materials. Next to instructors and other students, the most frequently mentioned dimension that assisted students in learning included such instructional materials as "a good textbook," "review" or "study guide sheets," "visual aids on overhead projectors," and "slides and films." The most frequently mentioned instructional aid, however, was lecture notes. On this campus the student publications office often hires graduate students experienced with the content of a particular large class, to attend lectures and take notes. Those notes are then typed and sold to students. Students suggested that "availability of lecture notes" was a major factor that assisted in their learning.

Comparisons of large classes with small classes suggested, then, that students perceived the instructors' effectiveness in teaching the subject matter, organization and clarity, and use of examples and illustrations to be of significantly higher quality in the best large classes. Instructors' interest in student learning and instructor-student interaction, however, were rated of significantly higher quality in the best small classes. Additional insights were obtained from students' ratings and responses related to the evaluation process in large classes.

Students' Perceptions of Evaluation Processes in Large Classes

Students' ratings of the evaluative and grading techniques in their best large and best small classes were not significantly different. Nevertheless, in response to open-ended questions, some perceived that grading in large classes was more "fair," "better," or "easier," because of "scoring on a curve," or "even distribution of grades." Others called for "better grading systems" and "fair" grading. Many evaluation comments focused on tests and homework.

Those who saw benefits to the tests in large classes focused on three major categories of perceptions about tests. Some students perceived that the content of tests in large classes assisted them in learning as tests were "more conceptual than technical," "more to the point," or "directly from the text." A second factor that students mentioned was the frequency of tests, suggesting that "weekly quizzes," "more than three tests," or "unit tests instead of a midterm and a final," could be used to motivate or "help students keep up." Others suggested that the increased test frequency would provide "more chances to see if you understand" and would decrease some of the stress. Another dimension that students mentioned in relation to testing was the availability of sample exams. A number of students suggested that they were assisted by "old exams," "back tests," "large test files," "somewhat the same tests," or "availability of old tests."

At least two dimensions related to testing showed little consensus in students' perceptions. One such dimension was the format of the test. Some students suggested that multiple-choice, objective tests, quizzes, and mark-sense tests assisted them in their learning of course content. Others, in making suggestions about how large classes might be improved, called for changes in test format with the elimination of true-false and multiple-choice items and the inclusion of more essay questions. In response to open-ended questions about what assisted or hindered their learning, a number of students addressed the issue of *cheating*. Some indicated that "cheating" assisted them in learning and a few even revealed that they were assisted by the opportunity "to cheat off such a large number of people." A number of students, however, suggested that provisions should be taken to decrease cheating. Many of the people in this latter category perceived that cheating "raised the curve" or "lowered my grade." Overall, there was a sense that in many large classes, "the tests are not adequate to measure learning."

On the dimension of reasonableness of assigned work, students' ratings of their best large class were significantly higher than their ratings for their best small class. Nevertheless, the way homework was used in large classes was not mentioned frequently in response to open-ended questions. A few students suggested that their learning in the large class was assisted by "lots of reading" or general "reading assignments." To the contrary, others suggested they were aided most by the fact that there is "less work," "no assignments turned in," or "only the vital assignments." Students who mentioned dimensions of homework as a hindrance suggested that they were hindered by "noncompelling, confusing reading," "lack of papers," "no daily assignments" or by the fact that "assigned work is all reading."

The students have provided a variety of insights to increase our understanding of large-class instruction. The perspectives reflected in these students' ratings of their best and worst large and small classes, have helped us to recognize that, on this campus, the best large classes can rival the best small classes on several instructional dimensions. In addition, the responses to open-ended comments have helped us to understand not only the instructional dimensions students perceive to be important but also the diversity in student opinions about those instructional dimensions.

Conclusion

Studying students' perceptions of large classes has helped us to understand how students interpret what happens in the large-class context. We find that data from the students' perceptions support our initial assumptions and provide insights about the dimensions of the teaching-learning process that students value in large classes.

First, the data reinforce our major assumption that teaching is, indeed, a complex process. Particularly in their responses to open-ended questions, students identified numerous dimensions in the large-class context that assisted or hindered their learning. They reinforced our view that large classes consist of complex interactions by suggesting that instructors, students, classroom atmosphere, and content were all factors that assisted or hindered their learning in large classes.

The students' perceptions also supported our second assumption that effective teaching requires a process of adaptation or adjustment. Probably the strongest support for this perspective was the variation in students' interpretations of the large-class context. From the results of this study, it is clear that students do not always agree about what assists or hinders their learning in large classes. Although there was strong consensus among students on some dimensions, such as instructor organization and clarity or quality of equipment, students disagreed on other dimensions, such as the quality of content in large classes or the kinds of tests. In addition, while some students were assisted by the presence of lots of other students, the low-pressure element, the sense of independence, and the accompanying attendance options, others felt their learning was hindered by many of the same factors. These results suggest that to be effective from the students' perspective, instructors must be prepared to adjust the instructional dimension that can address contrasting needs of students in large classes. Such adaptation requires weighing the trade-offs involved in adjusting certain dimensions and making decisions about ways to compensate for any adjustments. Instructors who wish to change to an essay test format, for instance, now know that they may be violating the preferences of students who like multiple-choice exams. The trade-off in changing test format, then, is an increase in satisfaction for some students and a decrease for others. The effective instructors seem to make decisions that will allow them to balance some of the dissatisfaction by increasing attention on other dimensions, thus meeting the needs of the dissatisfied students in other ways.

In a number of ways the data on students' perceptions of large classes supported our third assumption that students create their own interpretation and meaning about a particular instructional context. We found extensive variation in individual students' interpretations of what was happening in the large classes. While some saw the low-pressure atmosphere as an advantage that provided additional options, others clearly disliked the anonymity and impersonal nature of large classes. Further evidence of students' creating their own interpretation and meaning was the variation between overall student perceptions and perceptions of instructors and researchers who have previously examined the large-class context. Although researchers and instructors have often operated on the assumption that large classes are a reality that, at best, will be tolerated by students, these student data suggested that many students liked, and in some cases, preferred what they defined as large classes. Granted, the least satisfying experience is a poorly taught large class. Nevertheless, a majority of the students in this study preferred classes with enrollments of seventy-five or more. These findings challenge the importance of some of the instructional dimensions that, it has been argued, can only be achieved in classes with enrollments of twenty-five or fewer. Finally, the students' interpretation provided unique insights on the way some of the variables were perceived. For instance, the students attend both the large-class lecture and, if there is one, the corresponding small discussion section. They can, therefore, discuss the degree of consistency between content in the large lecture class and the discussion sections.

Other findings provided important insights into students' perceptions of large classes. Since, as previously stated, we believe that the balancing of many instructional dimensions determines the quality of large classes, we were not surprised that students most frequently mentioned that the professor assisted them in learning or that, on the dimension of instructor's effectiveness in teaching the course, their best large classes were as good or better than their best small classes. These findings reinforced our idea that in examining large classes, we might more successfully focus on the dimension of effective teaching than that of size. We were surprised to find, however, that the second most frequently mentioned dimension that assisted students in learning in large classes was other students. Such a finding suggests that large-class instructors may want to think about ways to capitalize on collaboration possibilities in the large-class context.

Foremost among the dimensions of large classes that hindered students' learning was the lack of instructor-student interaction with opportunities for questions and discussion. This finding is consistent with previous research that has suggested the great effect of class size in terms of such interaction (Marsh, Overall, and Kesler, 1979). The key seems to lie in finding ways to provide instructor-student interaction in the large-class context. Since students perceive quiz sections to be a primary factor in their learning in large classes, it may be that such discussion sessions can be used more extensively to fulfill the need for interaction. It is interesting to note, however, that in this study, even though students perceived that the quality of instructor-student interaction suffered in their best large classes, their ratings on that dimension were for the worst small class than for the best large class. Decreasing class size, then, does not necessarily mean that the quality of instructor-student interaction will increase.

The insights provided by examining the students' perceptions suggest that it is useful to incorporate the students' interpretations in our efforts to understand the teaching-learning process in the large class context. The students' perceptions reinforce our assumptions that teaching is a complex process that requires balancing a variety of instructional dimensions. Although we know that the instructor is ultimately responsible for decisions about course content, course objectives, use of course time, and evaluation procedures, we are convinced that knowing how students perceive large classes can assist in the decision-making process. We believe that instructors who have a more informed understanding of how students interpret their large-class experience can adjust a number of instructional dimensions to enhance the learning process in large classes for both themselves and students.

References

Feldman, K. A. "Class Size and College Students' Evaluations of Teachers and Courses: A Closer Look." *Research in Higher Education,* 1984, *21* (1), 45–116.

Marsh, H. W., Overall, J. U., and Kesler, S. P. "Class Size, Students' Evaluations, and Instructional Effectiveness." *American Educational Research Journal,* 1979, *16* (1), 57–70.

Nyquist, J. D., and Wulff, D. H. "The Training of Graduate Teaching Assistants at the University of Washington." In N. Chism (ed.), *Institutional Responsibilities and Responses in the Employment and Education of Teaching Assistants.* Columbus: Center for Teaching Excellence, Ohio State University, 1987.

Williams, D. D., Cook, P. F., Quinn, B., and Jensen, R. P. "University Class Size: Is Small Better?" *Research in Higher Education,* 1985, *23* (3), 307–318.

Donald H. Wulff is instructional development specialist at the Center for Instructional Development and Research, Jody D. Nyquist is lecturer in speech communication and director for instructional development at the Center for Instructional Development and Research, and Robert D. Abbott is professor in educational psychology and director for program research at the Center for Instructional Development and Research. All are at the University of Washington.

Although there is no one way to teach a class and no one style
that suits everyone, these are methods that have worked for me.

Six Keys to Effective Instruction in Large Classes: Advice from a Practitioner

J. Richard Aronson

There can be great satisfaction in teaching large classes. For twenty years I have taught classes with enrollments of up to seven hundred students and I have never tired of the experience. Mostly I enjoy the accomplishment of helping to start so many people simultaneously on the road to understanding my subject area. Large classes are very efficient and cost effective, but they can also be personal. There is no reason a teacher cannot build into the large lecture setting additional elements that provide individualized treatment to special student groups, especially those who need extra help or those who have developed a deeper interest in the subject.

I would like to suggest six keys to teaching the large class effectively. Although there is no one way to teach a class and no one style that suits everyone, these methods have worked for me and are directly addressed to a teacher facing a large class.

Key One: Don't Be Intimidated

Don't be intimidated by the size of the class. Once the class size passes fifty it does not make much difference how big it gets. You may

M. G. Weimer (ed.). *Teaching Large Classes Well.*
New Directions for Teaching and Learning, no. 32. San Francisco: Jossey-Bass, Winter 1987.

experience some nervousness in anticipation of meeting the group, but this is a natural and a healthy sign. In front of a large class you will face some of the same problems and sensations as does a performer; butterflies in the stomach, for example.

Fortunately, anticipatory nervousness provides the energy and the will to prepare your lecture in advance. It may be possible to wing it in a small class where you can rely on class questions to help you rephrase your presentation. But in the large lecture you have only one chance. If you are not expressing yourself well, you will lose the attention of your students. Soon you will see that distant look on their faces, or worse, you will hear heads hitting desks as students pass out from boredom.

Although you should recognize the importance of being interesting, you should not lose sight of the fact that your job is to teach, not entertain. You have to get a lot of material across, and quite often your course is a prerequisite for others. The goal you are striving for is to create an atmosphere where students are eager to learn more about your subject.

Incidentally, it is very important that on the first day of class you establish a good rapport with your students. Be sure to tell them your name (you would be shocked to learn how many students do not seem to know the names of their teachers). Also, spend some time telling them how you intend to run the class. Remove the ambiguity from such things as attendance requirements, seating arrangements, homework assignments, the number of exams, and even exam dates. Tell them how they can get in touch with you and with your teaching assistants. Also settle how you will determine their grades. Your remarks and a well-designed syllabus should get the course off to a good start.

Be a missionary. Not everybody in the lecture hall wants to be there or is interested in your subject at first. Show a little excitement and enthusiasm for your field. Explain why understanding your subject is essential for life-long happiness and fulfillment; why without your course you cannot be an interesting or attractive person. Whet their appetites for what is to come.

Key Two: Prepare Carefully

Prepare carefully for lectures. It is impossible to explain something that you yourself do not understand. I actually consider my preparation time a rehearsal. I know many scholars are offended when theatrical terms are applied to academic activities. We do not like to think we are in show business. Nevertheless, in the large lecture there is little if any chance to benefit from student reaction. What will make your lecture successful is not only what you say but how you say it. If your phrasing is ambiguous or hard to understand, if you mumble or slur your words, or if you have developed some peculiar nervous habits, the material you intended to cover in lecture may be lost. Preparing for lecture by just going over your notes is not good enough, especially when you are new at the game. It is not a bad idea to write out your lecture, not so that you might read it in class, which generally produces the deadliest of all lectures, but in order to see exactly what you can cover in fifty minutes. The best way to practice delivering a lecture is to deliver the lecture. But who will listen when no grades are at stake? You can practice in the shower, in front of the mirror, or in the car on the way to the university. The important thing is for you to actually hear the lecture you will deliver, to get your phrasing right, and to avoid fumbling for words. If you have television equipment at your disposal, taping a few lectures might be a good idea. I have never done this, however, because I am sure that I would be disgusted with the way I look. But if you are just starting out, risk humiliation and use the television equipment.

Key Three: Be Natural

It is dangerous to copy someone else's style. Don't tell jokes if you don't enjoy telling jokes. Humor is always a great asset and can be fantastically effective in teaching. But telling a joke for the sake of it, especially one that is not funny, can backfire. Just be natural and comfortable in front of the class. The university accommodates a wide variety of personalities and students enjoy the variety. So if you are the quiet type, be quiet; if you are the tough-guy type, be tough; and if you have a sense of humor by all means let it come out in class. Whatever your style, be sure to enjoy the experience.

Key Four: Be Personal

Even a large lecture can be personal. There are several vehicles for giving your students individual help. The usual method is the discussion group. It is common for large lecture classes to meet once a week in small groups. This gives the instructor a chance to get some student feedback and to understand better which parts of the material are troublesome. However, the discussion groups are usually run by teaching assistants with whom the lecturer must have a good working arrangement. Key Six discusses lecturer–teaching-assistant relations.

Other methods of achieving closer contact with your students include making yourself available to students immediately after lecture, making use of a computer network, and instituting a tutorial class, which I have affectionately called "The Loser's Club." Remaining in the lecture hall for a few minutes after class can do a lot to convince students that you are interested in them. One problem students have with large-class lectures is that they are anonymous. By remaining after class you can answer a few questions and show that you are accessible. You may also get a sense of what may have gone wrong with the lecture. Sometimes one bungled word or a mislabeled diagram can throw off one hundred students. They usually will not tell you when you have done something dumb in class, though they will remember it far longer than the material they are supposed to be learning. They may be afraid to speak up or they may get a kick out of watching you get deeper and deeper into trouble.

If your school has a computer network, you have another vehicle for personal communication. The computer can be an excellent teaching tool. Perhaps you can find an interactive teaching program that can be incorporated into your course. Self-teaching programs or problem sets and question-and-answer routines allow more advanced students to move at a faster pace to a higher level of understanding. The network also offers a method of direct and immediate communication with each student. It can be used to organize homework assignments or simply to send messages.

Another way to get closer to your students and to protect those who are not doing so well or not living up their own expectations is through the "Loser's Club." A number of years ago a student came up to me after the first lecture of the semester and very politely said, "Hi Professor Aronson, I'm here again. It's my third try, but this time I'm going to pass." I was depressed to think that not only could a student flunk my course twice but, even worse, that I wasn't even aware of it. At that moment I invented the Loser's Club.

The club is a tutorial that meets on a weekly basis throughout the semester. At Lehigh undergraduates are permitted to serve as apprentice teachers. Each semester I select one or two outstanding undergraduate majors in the College of Business and Economics to serve in this capacity. Each week they hold question-and-answer sessions with students seeking extra help.

Attendance at the "Loser's Club" is never compulsory but I constantly remind students who are repeating the class or who have done poorly on an hour exam to attend. It will come as no surprise that the students who get the most out of the experience are the tutors themselves. But I monitor the process and remain convinced that the students in need also gain much. I also encourage all students performing below their own expectations to join. I have found the club to be useful to those eager and hardworking students who need just a bit more help in getting to the B or A level.

I might also mention that care must be taken in calling this class the "Loser's Club." It is, of course, done to make light of the problem. If you decide to use such a blatant title, be sure to make a little joke about it. Some students are very sensitive and are fearful of being labeled "losers." Occasionally I've called it the "opportunity class" or the "special tutorial," but I keep coming back to its original name.

Key Five: Prevent Students from Feeling Insignificant and Anonymous

The law of large classes is that each individual feels insignificant and anonymous. Students sitting at the rear of the hall believe that they are out of your sight and hearing range. They also believe that if you don't know that they missed a class it won't have an effect on their grade and achievement in the course. Such problems will be compounded if you are lucky enough to have your class scheduled for 8 A.M.

The best and perhaps only way to keep your students interested in the subject is to deliver stimulating and exciting lectures. But how can you keep the interest of a student who has not come to class or who is asleep before the lecture has started? I have been living on campus for three years as faculty master of a residential college, and have been impressed with the hours students keep. Most students do not live normal lives. The lights of our building burn continuously and many students do not get to bed until 2 or 3 in the morning—and it's not all studying. This makes it very difficult for them to be alive at 8 A.M. I have found two solutions for this problem: the cordless microphone and the "curve buster."

The cordless microphone allows me to wander anywhere I wish while lecturing. I lecture from the front of the class, which is normal, or from the back. I can lecture from any seat in the hall or from outside the hall. Such moving around tends to keep the students awake. At a recent 8 A.M. lecture a young woman had fallen asleep in her seat. (I presume she was asleep before the lecture started.) Since the seat next to her was vacant I sat down and continued to lecture from that position. I even took some notes for her. Needless to say, when she awoke she was a little disoriented. I have kept an eye on her. She is in class every morning; she is wide awake and she smiles. I think she knows I care about her performance.

The "curve buster" is a device for maintaining class morale. It provides students with an opportunity to improve their grades by answering extra credit questions that are administered during lecture hour. CBs, as they are called, are unannounced. Sometimes I give a curve buster at the start of class and sometimes at the end. Curve busters take only about ten minutes to administer. Sometimes they are problems; sometimes they are multiple-choice questions. Three variations are run simultaneously to keep everyone honest. Curve buster points are aggregated and taken into consideration in setting a student's grade, which is determined in a two-step fashion. The original distribution is determined by the scores on the hour exams and the final. Then boundaries are set for letter grades. Next we add the curve buster points. This allows students near grade boundaries to improve their letter grades. Curve busters have encouraged students to come to class and, more important, to keep up with their work. The curve buster problem usually tests material covered during the previous hour or in the current lecture. It is joyously accepted as a device that can only help and not hurt a student's grade.

Key Six: Stay in Touch with TAs

Teaching assistants can make or break your class, so it is important to know what they are doing and how the students are reacting to them. I do not believe in overtraining TAs or even in observing their classes. I feel that they too must develop their own style and that they should be as independent as possible. As teachers-in-training, the sooner they understand that they are responsible for the success of their classes, the better. TAs must attend all lectures, which provides them with material for their own classes. They not only see what I covered but how I covered it. I may have been particularly obscure on some points. Good TAs tell you when you have been ineffective. They are encouraged to use any style they want, to use homework assignments if they want, and to keep regular office hours. I want my TAs to get as close to the students as possible. Students hesitate to approach the lecturer of a large class. A good TA can usually develop a closer working relationship with a student than can the professor of a large class. Incidentally, I do not let the TAs see advance copies of the hour exams. This frees them to work with students to outfox the professor.

Lehigh University runs a summer prep program for TAs. In this brief training program each student works in front of a TV camera and participates in discussions with several professors and TAs who have already served for a year or two. The program has proven successful, especially for many of our foreign-born graduate students for whom English is a second language. During the semester I meet with my TAs and apprentice teachers on a weekly basis. These meetings are for discussing problems they might experience and for exchanging ideas on what to bring up in class or how to assign homework. With those who run the Loser's Club we keep track of those individuals who are receiving or are in need of extra help.

The TAs play an important role in determining each student's grade. The distribution of grades is first set by points accumulated on hour exams, the final exam, and the curve busters. A large number of students land on the border between one grade and another. The TAs have the power to push a student over or under the line. The over-and-under procedure is carried out with all TAs present, which helps us provide fairly good inter-discussion group uniformity in setting grades. We know that the TA experience varies from person to person and we know that some TAs tend to be easier graders than others. Since we set the grades with all the TAs present, we can aim for fairness.

Conclusion

Teaching the large class is an important responsibility for which there is great satisfaction and reward. If you are successful you will have influenced the lives and thoughts of a great number of people, and you will have made it possible for your department to offer a wider selection of courses. Most of all, you will notice that your colleagues will treat you with great care, admiration, and respect. Why? Because they want you to keep teaching the course. They all harbor the fear that should you decide to move on to something else, they will be next. So enjoy the experience and wear the position well.

J. Richard Aronson is William L. Clayton Professor of Business and Economics and director of the Fairchild-Martindale Center for the Study of Private Enterprise at Lehigh University.

From my experience two areas of detail are keys to success in the large course; adequately prepare before the course begins, and remain aware of the pulse of the class throughout the semester.

Dealing with Details in a Large Class

Robert P. Brooks

Teaching a large class well is challenging to even the most resourceful instructor. Potential problems abound, but many of these can be avoided by paying attention to a whole variety of details. Some potential problems can be avoided by taking care of details before the course begins. Not all of the potential problems associated with large classes are guaranteed to arise. But the details regarding how you will respond should be worked out as you plan for the course. This chapter identifies a variety of potential problems, but more important, it offers a set of suggestions that can make your large classes function as well or better than a course enrolling far fewer students.

The Problems You Can Plan For

Many of the logistics and problems of teaching a large class can be solved by good preparation before you enter the classroom on the first day. Potential problems can be anticipated. It is difficult, though not

Appreciation is extended to Bruce A. Murphy, associate professor of political science at Pennsylvania State University, for his enlightening discussions on teaching a large class.

M. G. Weimer (ed.). *Teaching Large Classes Well.*
New Directions for Teaching and Learning, no. 32. San Francisco: Jossey-Bass, Winter 1987.

39

impossible, to recover from a mistake made in front of one hundred or more students. This is certainly true of any teaching activity, but unpreparedness and poor organization tend to become magnified in a large class.

The logistics of successfully teaching a large class take time. By expending extra effort ahead of time, the chances of a major disaster occurring are greatly reduced. This preparedness will undoubtedly result in a controlled classroom environment where one's level of confidence is increased and the framework for learning is solid.

Let's look at some specific pre-class plans that will prevent trouble. I believe that the most crucial element is a detailed and organized syllabus. You cannot prepare a detailed syllabus without that process contributing to the overall organization of the course. The syllabus should include a schedule of lecture topics, preferably specifying the date of presentation. Readings from texts and library material should also be similarly detailed. Beyond this basic structure, I would recommend that the first page of the syllabus discuss course objectives and list office locations and hours for both the instructor and teaching assistants. Paragraphs on grading policy (for example, whether make-up exams are allowed, whether tests are cumulative, and whether surprise quizzes are a possibility) and course rules (such as, attendance expectations, how tests will be administered, and adherence to assignment due dates) are recommended. A well-designed syllabus does not mean there is no flexibility; lecture topics can always be shifted by a few days to take advantage of an opportunity, such as a prominent guest lecturer. It does mean that students understand what is expected of them, which means fewer trivial questions asked of the instructor.

For those who use methods other than the traditional lecture, careful planning of course logistics is important. I teach a lecture/laboratory course that involves guest lecturers, a variety of audiovisual media, and buses to be scheduled for field trips. At least two months in advance I confirm dates for speakers, order films and projectionists, visit potential sites for field trips, and make sure buses are available at the right place for the correct amount of time. A lecture or laboratory that runs smoothly helps to promote learning. Conversely, watching slides upside down or spending an hour in the rain waiting for a bus, although sometimes humorous, more often detracts from the learning experience.

I always visit the classroom before the first lecture. It makes me feel more comfortable. I can familiarize myself with the podium, the lights, the audiovisual services, and make any necessary corrections before the first class. You may want to try out your transparencies and write on the blackboard to be sure the material is visible everywhere in the room. I do not hesitate to request a room change if I find it necessary.

Getting the Class Started Right

Your performance on the first day of class sets the stage for the remainder of the course. The importance of how you present yourself and the expectations you set for students during the first class meeting should not be underestimated. Step one is to give the impression of confidence and control, even if your heart is pounding and your stomach is queasy. Your course will be run as you see fit, but at the same time you need to project an honest concern, for the student's welfare.

In my class of about one hundred students, I begin with being on time. I do not encourage latecomers by being late myself. I begin by introducing myself. Students appreciate knowing something about the instructor beyond a name and office number. I let them know how many times the course has been taught, what changes have been made from the previous time it was taught (especially if students recommended the changes), where I went to school, what I majored in, and what demands there are on my time (such as research, administration, and other courses). In the future, I plan to hand out a professor profile patterned after a famous advertisement for Scotch to humorously provide some of this information.

Next, I go over the syllabus in detail. Taking fifteen to twenty minutes to talk about the course, I describe the type of tests I give, and discuss the nature of and rationale for required assignments. I introduce the TAs for the course and ask if there are any questions. Finding out about student expectations for the course helps stimulate discussion later on when the subject matter is more difficult.

At most, I give fifteen minutes of actual lecture material, just to break the ice. With this approach, when the class meets next, they will know me, my lecture style, the topic for the day, and what is expected of them. To me, this approach makes both the instructor and students comfortable in a rigorously controlled, fairly impersonal environment.

Details of Classroom Management and Control

Discipline. Most discipline problems in the classroom are simple nuisances or distractions. There are a few instances when, during a full moon, a student loses his or her inhibitions and publicly challenges the instructor's authority. The way in which an instructor responds to these challenges in large measure determines how many and how serious subsequent ones will be. If an altercation with a student occurs, do not play out the confrontation before two hundred interested onlookers. If the answer you give does not satisfy the student, stop trying and suggest that the two of you meet after class to discuss the issue.

By exhibiting certain exemplary behaviors, an instructor can virtually eliminate the truly disruptive behavior of a few troublesome individuals. If the instructor sets the appropriate tone from the first day, most disciplinary and logistical problems can be avoided. Despite my emphasis on control, I still maintain an informal and pleasant atmosphere in class that encourages frequent interaction.

An instructor of a large class must be confident (or perceived as being confident), not arrogant, just assured of his or her abilities. However, to manage a large class constructively, instructors need some previous teaching experience. Administrators should give inexperienced teachers a chance to develop their particular style without the added pressures of large numbers of students. Having a first teaching experience in a department's introductory large-enrollment course is not the easiest way to begin a college teaching experience.

As mentioned, organization and preparedness promote confidence, and hopefully help the instructor gain student respect. A few areas where even confidence may not be enough and some directed action is needed are discussed below.

Punctuality. Latecomers can be distracting to both the instructor's train of thought and to student attentiveness. With large classes, it seems that someone is always arriving late or leaving early. You can't eliminate this entirely, but you can minimize it. A punctual instructor who arrives a few minutes early to set up and begins promptly sets a good example. When you are unavoidably late, apologize quickly and briefly, and assume immediate control. Be on time. It is difficult enough to get the attention of several hundred people without beginning with an apology.

Indicate from the outset that tardiness is unacceptable. Use a glance, a dramatic pause, or verbalize your concern early in the semester. Do not hope the problem will go away and then respond out of aggravation. By then the habit of being late is well-ingrained.

Attentiveness. In a large class, lack of contact between an instructor and students can lead to inattentiveness. Eye contact is difficult. The instructor seems impersonal, distant, and removed. An instructor must be sensitive to the level of attentiveness within the class. For example, you are in a technical section of a lecture. Your voice drones on as you wade through the material. Suddenly you hear yourself being boring. You sense a remoteness between yourself and the class. Solution? At the very least, alter the tone of your voice, ask a question, or tell a joke. Learn to listen to your own instincts. Recognize when your hold on their attention is weakening, and react immediately.

Sometimes the physical nature of the classroom or the timing of the class is not conducive to maintaining student interest. Maybe it's too warm, too dark, too early, or after lunch. Open the windows. Change the lighting. Request a room change for subsequent semesters. Lecture from a different location. Change the routine. If things are not working, start afresh. If you are aware and willing to admit when student interest is declining, you are more than halfway to finding a solution.

Cheating. Most institutions have a written policy or honor code that addresses cheating. It should not be tolerated. It may be necessary with a large class to give an initial warning before the first quiz or exam.

On the day of the exam, part of the warning might be a clear description of the behaviors an instructor considers to be cheating. Some studies have shown that instructors and student definitions do not always agree. Comments such as "Please keep your eyes on your own papers. If you must look around, look forward," or "Please space yourselves evenly throughout the classroom," will draw attention to your concern and awareness of the problem, without badgering the honest majority. When students must take exams in close quarters, the instructor should prepare several versions of a test that have the same questions, but in different order, thus eliminating the advantage of the roving eye. While proctoring exams, the instructors or TAs should circulate within the classroom to answer questions and to intimidate potential cheaters. Avoid doing other work (such as reading or grading lab reports) while proctoring, so you can gaze or walk around frequently. Cheating is made easier when only a single answer is correct. Design assignments that reward the innovations of individuals, such as creative writing or finding unique solutions to hypothetical problems. Ideally, exams and assignments should be designed to make cheating impractical and worthless, although this is difficult.

Miscellany. With regard to questioning and testing strategies within a large class, a few additional suggestions follow. During a lecture when all that appears in the audience are blank stares I stop, abandon the notes, and ask questions about what I had been discussing. I try to find out what they know and what they don't know. This substitutes as a quiz without grades, offers an opportunity to interact with students for a short period of time, and provides feedback on the course's progress. If the results are good, I congratulate students; if the results suggest some confusion, then I briefly review the information in question. When I ask questions about the text or assigned readings and it is obvious that students have slacked off, I tell them that I will ask that question again during the next class period (and I do). That source of potential embarrassment will usually motivate most students to catch up. I prefer to go over exams in class, but I do so in a general way that summarizes some of the poorly answered questions. To avoid embarrassing students, I do not entertain questions about a student's specific exam, but encourage meeting with individuals after class or at another time. Although I try not to have misleading or ambiguous questions on an exam, if one is missed by the majority of the class, I will calculate grades without it rather than respond to individual queries ad infinitum.

44

I am sure there are many other worthy solutions to handling the logistics of a large class. From my experience, the two key points are to adequately prepare before the course begins, and to remain aware of the pulse of the class throughout the semester. Teaching a large class need not be an intimidating experience. Rather, it should be a rewarding experience for both the instructor and the students.

Robert P. Brooks is associate professor of wildlife ecology in the School of Forest Resources at Pennsylvania State University.

The challenge is to reconcile the recommendations of the experts for involved learning with the reality of passivity that plagues large classes.

Student Involvement: Active Learning in Large Classes

Peter J. Frederick

> *Tell me, and I'll listen.*
> *Show me, and I'll understand.*
> *Involve me, and I'll learn.*
> *—Teton Lakota Indian*

Most college teachers have had the distressing experience at the end of a brilliant lecture of asking students, "any questions?" only to be greeted with deafening silence. However effective one's presentational style and ability to communicate, student passivity remains a learning problem in large impersonal lecture courses. Increasing student involvement through making greater use of active modes of teaching was the major recommendation of the National Institute of Education report in 1984, *Involvement in Learning: Realizing the Potential of American Higher Education.* Nearly all learning theorists, faculty development consultants, and reports on higher education recommend the importance of interactive, participatory student involvement for learning that affects cognitive and affective growth. As Dunham and Gleason (1984, p. 50) have put it, "instructional environments need to be intimate, interactive, and investigative."

M. G. Weimer (ed.). *Teaching Large Classes Well.*
New Directions for Teaching and Learning, no. 32. San Francisco: Jossey-Bass, Winter 1987.

Yet despite these recommendations, most college and university professors in most classes most of the time continue to lecture. Even those who write articles on the importance of interaction and discussion, still lecture more than is recommended. The lecture persists for all kinds of reasons. "I'd like to do less lecturing, but I've got too much to cover." Or, "That's all right for you but in my field I have to lecture to get them ready for the 300 level course." Or, "I'd like to try some new ideas, but I can't—I have three hundred students in the class, you know." Or, "Student interaction is impossible in my classroom. The chairs are in rows bolted to the floor—all I can do is lecture."

I believe that these genuine expressions of concern need not be barriers to active learning. The challenge is to reconcile the experts' recommendations about learning with the reality of the passivity that plagues large classes. This chapter will suggest several specific, practical ways of promoting active, participatory learning within the large lecture class format. Each of these approaches assumes a class size of at least one hundred students, sitting in conventionally tiered, dimly-lit lecture halls, with chairs in rows bolted to the floor facing a professor up (or down) front behind a lectern. Each of these strategies is applicable to fields of widely diverse content. The goal is to help faculty members discover ways of achieving an interactive, investigatory, and even intimate learning environment in large impersonal settings, thus empowering their students to take responsibility for their own learning.

Fundamental to each approach are three interrelated pervasive themes that I believe are crucial in promoting active learning. First, given diverse student learning styles, teachers should use a variety of strategies for teaching and learning, not only on different days but also within any single class period. In other words, there should be energy shifts within a class about every twenty minutes by changing both the activity and the voice or voices that speak. Second, in classes of any size, but especially large ones, visual reinforcements (on blackboards, handouts, or overhead transparencies) are vital in order to focus attention and clarify the context of verbal presentations, especially for those increasing numbers of students who are field-dependent and visual rather than auditory learners. And third, students learn best when there are spaces in the content being developed or explained on any given day. If instructors provide holes in their lectures, students must fill the space with their own insights, reading, analysis, or connections. Students learn best when they are involved in ownership of their intellectual discoveries, especially those that hook into their own experiences.

The active learning suggestions of this chapter are grouped into five sections: interactive lectures; questioning; using small groups in large classes; critical-thinking and problem-solving exercises; and large-class debates, simulations, and role playing.

Interactive Lectures

One form of the interactive, or participatory, lecture involves brainstorming. Students are invited to help create a lecture by participating in the process of ordering a topic into a coherent, rational pattern. When beginning a new topic, instructors may start with a participatory lecture by asking students to call out "everything you know or think you know about World War I" (or Freud, Darwinism, China, management principles, the Renaissance, DNA, or whatever). As recorded on an overhead transparency or blackboard, a list of specific names, dates, and events; descriptions of natural phenomena and human experience; feelings and prejudices; and possibly even interpretive judgments will unfold. Students bring to most courses both a degree of familiarity and considerable misinformation. Since anything goes brainstorming provides an opportunity for many students to participate and for faculty to find out what students already know and do not know.

The only rule of brainstorming is to acknowledge every offering by writing it down, thus providing visual reinforcement and honoring student contributions. As ideas are proposed, clever teachers might arrange the ideas in rough groupings. Alternatively, they might ask students to suggest categories and to comment on the accuracy and relative importance of the array of events, experiences, and interpretations. Refinements can be dealt with by erasures, a luxury not allowed in the formal lecture. Thus begins a jointly created coherent understanding of the topic.

In an interactive session like this it is necessary, as in any lecture, for the professor to have a clear idea what should be revealed and discovered in the process. Some points, probably, must be made. At the same time, however, teachers must guard against excessive manipulation and be flexible enough to depart from their preconceived ideas. The final creation should legitimately reflect both student and teacher conceptions of what is important about a topic. When the class is over, the teacher and students will have created an organized configuration of salient points and concepts. In this interactive process, students spend more time thinking than recording as they concentrate on contributing to the evolving lecture before them.

Obviously, the participatory lecture can be done badly. When students have not brought to the class the limited knowledge provided by their prior experience or reading, or when the professor manipulates student statements to a rigidly preconceived schema, the experience can be dreary. But when the mutual participation is free and open, students are actively engaged and teachers might even gain new insights about familiar material. Although less efficient than a traditional lecture, the participatory lecture actively involves many students and can be done in any size auditorium.

A variation of the interactive lecture is to ask students at the beginning of class to call out one concrete visual image that stands out from a text, scene, laboratory experiment, event, art object, or personal experience. "From your reading of *The Color Purple* (or *Candide,* or an account of Galileo's trials, or a surgical procedure), what one specific scene or moment stands out in your mind?" Spending a few minutes hearing these images at the beginning of a traditional lecture (or in the middle somewhere) activates student energy and enhances the vividness of the day's content. No analysis is necessary—just recollections and brief description. The recall of concrete scenes prompts further recollections, and a flood of images flows from the students. As students report their images, the instructor list them on a transparency or blackboard, thus providing a visual backdrop to the lecture or discussion that follows. After five minutes, ask the class: "What themes seem to emerge from these items? What connects these images? Is there a pattern to our recollected events? What is missing?" In this inductive approach, facts precede analysis. Many students get to say something early in class and every contribution gets written down to aid the collective memory and provide a visual reinforcement to learning.

Another way to introduce a new topic—or to check on learning halfway through one—is to ask students to suggest statements they think are true about some particular issue. "It is true about deregulation that . . ." "We have agreed that it is true about the welfare system that . . ." "It is true about the theory of relativity that . . ." and so on. I have found this strategy useful for dealing with a topic—slavery, for example—where students think they already know a great deal but the accuracy of their assumptions demands examination. This exercise reveals the complexity and ambiguity of knowledge as students present their truth statements and other students raise questions about or refute them. It also generates a list of questions and of issues demanding further study.

Using Questions for Involvement

The use of questions—for students and for instructors—is an obvious way to shifting energy back and forth in large classes. Teachers ask rhetorical questions all the time in lectures. But they also ask real ones and expect responses. There are several approaches.

From the movie *Paper Chase* we all have an indelibly stereotyped view of one method of asking questions in large classes. One student is singled out and interrogated unmercifully in order to tease out the significance of a particular legal case. When I watch John Houseman at work in his role as the pitiless law professor, I always think of Socrates, who was a mixture of great teacher genuinely guiding others to their own self-discoveries and skillful, manipulative, intellectual hustler steering others to his desired answers. Having admitted that, we can do variations of the same approach, presumably more mercifully than either Houseman or Socrates.

One approach is to address a somewhat open-ended question to the class: "What were the causes of World War I?" Or, "what is the meaning of the green light at the end of Daisy's dock?" Or, "how did the universe begin?" Or, "what is art?" Or even, "why was Socrates condemned to death?" A student answer is met with a follow-up question, which is directed at the class generally. The instructor need not put one person on the spot, for the primary point is to convey substantive content and raise further questions. In the end, as in brainstorming, a number of points and arguments are articulated and perhaps even listed on the board. A further question can invite the students to begin to critically analyze the various arguments. "Which of these arguments makes the most sense to you, and why?"

A second approach to questioning, perhaps the next step, is to put a question to the class and ask three students sitting next to one another to explore it for five minutes. "What were Austria's problems?" "Should art be socially useful?" "Would you have voted for Socrates' death? Why or why not?" The best kinds of questions are those not simply seeking information (Austria) but those requiring students to make judgments and choices among equally compelling alternatives (Socrates). After only five minutes in the trios, enormous energy is generated by putting the choice to the class: "How many would have voted to put Socrates to death?" "How many not?" "Why?" A lecturer could indeed have presented both the pertinent information and alternatives more efficiently but without the interaction, dispersal of energy, and multiplicity of voices, points of view, and controversy.

But students also have their questions and even in large classes we can provide ways for them to ask questions and learn how to formulate better ones. Being able to ask questions about a particular text or issue is essential in coming to terms with it. There are many ways of generating student questions. Ask students ahead of time (on Wednesday for Friday's class) to prepare one or two questions about their reading or a topic and bring them to class. Instructors can put the assignment to them this way: "A question I still have about slavery (or Kant, the New Deal, quarks, mammography, Gilligan's stages of moral development, or whatever) but have been afraid to ask, is . . ." Students can either walk into Friday's class with their questions or be invited to put them on cards and submit them ahead of time, a technique which helps reticent students' questions to be heard.

Another variation is to ask students as they enter the classroom to call out questions about the text or topic they hope will be answered that day. At the end of the hour ask them to write down one or two still unre-solved questions they want explored at the next class. Or, at some point halfway through a period divide the class into pairs or small groups of three or four and ask them to "take five minutes to agree on one question that you think is crucial that I respond to." This will sort out fewer, more thoughtful questions. In addition, and equally important, this task leads to some peer teaching and learning as one member of a group answers another's question in the course of the search for a consensus question. Hearing student questions is an excellent way, in addition to brief, one-minute written reports, for a professor to get feedback on how well students are learning. The quality and substance of their questions indicates areas of strength and gaps in understanding.

A *press conference* is a questioning variation that is well-suited to concluding a unit. Students are invited, as investigative reporters, to ask questions of their teacher about the topic they have been studying. They may seek to clarify confusing material or to find out new information or, like a budding Socrates or Mike Wallace, to press their professor's posi-tion on an issue to a point of contradiction or inadequate evidence. The teacher's responses might be crisp and short or might constitute mini-lectures. Professors can structure questioning sessions in any number of imaginative ways to facilitate and humanize the learning process. In any event, this lecture-hall variation is feasible in any size class; it succeeds in providing interaction, energy shifts, and different voices; and it underlines the importance of students' responsibility for their own learning.

Small Groups in Large Classes

The suggestions already made indicate the importance of breaking large classes into small groups. Whether the class size is 50, 150, or 500, it can always be broken down into smaller groups of five, eight, ten, or whatever, thus serving many purposes. The first, quite simply, is to pro-vide energy and interaction, enabling more students to think during class, to say something, and to generate more ideas about a text or topic. Groups usually lend themselves to a lively, competitive spirit, whether asked to or not. Students in groups are inevitably interested not only in their own group but also in "what they're doing over there." Moreover, there is potentially more intimacy in the class when broken into groups. Not only do students get to know each other but the teachers have an opportunity to establish personal contact with more students as they move around listening to a sampling of the small group discussions. Furthermore, reticent students find it easier to express themselves in the smaller groups and can gain some confidence in speaking up in larger settings after having practiced talking to a smaller, safer audience.

There are three crucial points to consider in helping small groups to work and learn efficiently. First, the instructions should be clear, simple, and task oriented, such as the following examples. "Decide together which of the brothers is the major character in the novel." "Why did the experiment fail and what would you suggest changing?" "What is Picasso's painting saying?" "Identify three positive and three negative qualities of King David's character." "If you were the company treasurer (or lawyer), what decision would you make?" "If you were Lincoln, what would you do about Fort Sumter?"

The second necessity in giving instructions is to give the groups a sense of how much time they have to do their work as in, "Take ten minutes to define your group's position." And third, instructors should be sure to ask each group to select a recorder and to provide ways of reporting back and debriefing the process. In not-so-large classes, one way is to invite each group briefly to state their conclusion(s) orally in turn, with the teacher recording them on the board. Another is to ask the recorder from each group to write its conclusions on a transparency or on newsprint posted around the room. Still another, accompanied by brief oral presentations, is to write them down on paper to be collected, collated, and reported back by the teacher at the next class.

In very large lecture halls filled with 200–400 students, breaking up into small groups is more difficult but still possible. At an appropriate point, interrupt your lecture to ask two or three students sitting next to each other to discuss an issue or question together for a few minutes. "What's the most important point I've been making for the past ten minutes?" Who is the real hero of the story?" "What's the major constitutional concern in this case?" "What's the answer to the problem?'" After as little as three or four minutes, invite volunteers to stand and report conclusions and concerns.

This process provides public affirmation of the thinking of a room full of students, thus giving feedback both to other students and to the teacher on how well they understand a particular topic. Even "wrong" feedback is instructive and can dictate the next appropriate minilecture and reading assignment. Without this short break, the professor might not have known the gaps in student knowledge and gone ahead into the next unit, at the cost of losing a good portion of the class. Moreover, with even brief shifts of energy, students not only experience a variety of voices and a sense of shared responsibility for their learning but also wake up and are more likely to listen attentively to the teacher's next twenty minutes of lecturing.

Problem Solving and Critical Thinking

These suggestions have been predicated upon shifts of energy and voice in about twenty-minute blocks of time, a form of arranging the information to facilitate comprehension and memory. A typical fifty-minute class period, therefore, should usually involve three segments. First, the instructor delivers a twenty-minute lecture, perhaps explaining a new concept, or presenting a case study, or otherwise setting the stage for some activity involving students. Then students participate for fifteen to twenty minutes, practicing the new concept, discussing the implications of a problem, or role-playing the effects of a situation the professor has described in the opening minilecture. After some feedback on the activity, the professor concludes the class by summarizing the important points, re-explaining the concept, and bringing closure to the class. Alternatively, teachers might use the last ten minutes to prepare students for an out-of-class assignment or to introduce a new topic.

This alternating approach is applicable for any discipline, perhaps best for natural and social science fields where instruction calls for a mixture of theory and data, model and findings, or hypothesis and experimental demonstration. In these situations, each involving questions of how best to proceed after learning a theory or model, students are trained in critical thinking and problem-solving skills. "How could the nation experience rapid inflation and high unemployment at the same time?" "Why does the electron in some experiments behave like a particle and in others like a wave?" "How come the circle cannot be squared?" "If I can generate heat energy in an object, why can't I use heat from it to run my machine?" "Why do some of us perceive an old woman and others a young one?" "What brought Captain Parker's men to Lexington Green that cold April morning?"

The problem-solving lecture begins with a question, a paradox, an enigma, or a compellingly unfinished human story—some tantalizing problem that hooks student interest. The answer unfolds during the class hour; if the instructor is skillful, the unfolding will be completed with only about ten or fewer minutes left in the period. Solving the problem, depending on what it is or in what field, may require a scientific demonstration, a mathematical proof, an economic model, the outcome of the novel's plot, or historical narrative. Solving problems is an ideal way of breaking a class period into alternating chunks of time and dispersed energy.

The problem, or question, is woven throughout the lecture, inviting students to fill in spaces in the story or model with their own unfolding solutions to the problem as they listen. Preferably, the resolution could be an interactive process in which students' tentative solutions to a problem or completions of a story, are elicited, listed on the board, and discussed. "What do you think will happen?" "Which solution, outcome, or explanation makes the most sense to you?" If no consensus, the teacher lectures a little more, invites a new set of student responses, and asks the question again. Ideally, when the problem is finally resolved, most students will have figured it out themselves just before the teacher's solution is announced at the class-ending bell.

The large-class lecture setting also provides an opportunity to practice an old-fashioned but woefully ignored technique: explication de texte. Instructors can teach students how to read, even in large-lecture classes, by going directly to a text and reading and analyzing passages together out loud. At first, the professor models how to read and interpret a passage. The students, following along in their books (or on handouts or an overhead projection), observe the professor working through a selection from a speech, sermon, essay, poem, or fictional passage. In introductory survey courses I regularly spend part of a class period early in the term showing how I would read and highlight a traditional textbook.

Then it is their turn: how better for students to develop their reading skills than to see them modeled, followed by an opportunity to practice analyzing a text themselves? There are many ways to select appropriate passages and structure such a class. Invite students, either ahead of time or at the start of class, to "find one or two quotations from the text which you found particularly significant," or, "find one quotation you especially liked and one you especially disliked," or, "identify a quotation which you think best illustrates the major thesis of the chapter," or, "find a quotation which suggests, to you, the key thematic symbol of the text."

Students are then ready to read these passages out loud and discuss them. "Jennifer, would you please read the top paragraph on page 144?" Be sure to pause long enough for everyone to find the right spot in their book: "Top of page 144—is everyone with us?" Lively and illuminating engagement is guaranteed because not all students select the same quotations nor, probably, do they all interpret passages the same way. Upon reaching a particularly ambiguous passage, small groups of three to four students could be asked to struggle with the meaning. "Three of you sitting next to each other: put your heads together and in your own words state what you think is the main point of the passage." Or, "what's happening here?" Teachers may invite a few groups to report their reflections, giving teachers an opportunity to react to the substance of their interpretation, comparing it to their own thoughts. Breaking into small groups disperses the energy and provides practice and feedback for students before returning again to the professor's voice and analysis. After having struggled with a passage themselves for a few minutes, hearing the teacher's interpretation has more meaning.

This process of modeling how to read analytically, followed by practice, assessment, and more modeling can be done in large-lecture classes for other than just verbal texts. Art historians, musicologists, economists, and anthropologists have traditionally used lectures to demonstrate how to "read" an abstract painting, sonata allegro form, supply and demand curve, or artifact. Natural scientists explain their texts with elaborate demonstrations. Some social science teachers use the lecture period to train students in other analytical skills: quantitative analysis of graphs, charts, tables, and census data, as well as how to read maps. I regularly hand out short historical documents in my classes—a household inventory, a diary entry, a census table, a folk tale, a ship's manifest, an old tool, a family photograph—and ask: "what do you see?" Then, after hearing several descriptions: "what does it mean? what implications can you draw from the document on how people lived?"

Whether using traditional verbal or nontraditional sources, and whether working with forty or four hundred students, the large class is an opportunity to teach critical-analysis and reading skills to our students. The process of participating together in the analysis of a common text is interactive, investigatory, and intimate. To summarize: instructors can make sure students have a copy of the source in question in front of them (or visual access through slides and overhead transparencies), and the follow the three steps of modeling by the instructor, practice by the students, and feedback.

Whole Class Debates, Simulations, and Role Playing

Although assigning specific tasks to small groups of students can disperse energy and achieve interaction in large classes, not all instructors are comfortable with the uncertainty and potential lack of control implicit in the decentralized large class. Therefore, I would like to suggest a few ways of achieving more student participation and engagement in large classes without changing the professor's central controlling role in the classroom.

One strategy is to take advantage of the central aisle dividing large lecture halls in order to structure debates. Students can either support the side of an issue assigned to the half of the hall where they happen to be sitting, or as prearranged, can come to class prepared to take a seat on one particular side of a debate. I put up signs over the lecture hall doors labeling the two sides. Although neither one of two polar sides of an issue contains the whole truth, it is pedagogically energizing (if only to point out the complexity of truth) for students to be compelled to choose and then to defend one side of a dichotomous question.

The following process permits the professor to maintain rigorous control from the podium in leading the debate: "From the right side of the hall we will hear five statements on behalf of the hawk side of U.S. involvement in Vietnam, after which we will hear five statements from the left on behalf of the dove side." The process can be repeated, including rebuttals, before concluding by asking for two or three volunteers to make summary arguments for each side. Other obvious debate topics, following the stimulus of a reading, film, or minilecture, include such questions as: "Should Nora have left or stayed?" "Burke or Paine?" "Abortion: pro-life or pro-choice?" "Marx or Adam Smith?" "Intervene in Nicaragua or not?" "Evolution or creationism?"

But of course, most important questions do not divide into halves. Our good students would never settle for forced dichotomous choices. When some students (quite rightly) refuse to choose one side or the other, create a middle ground and space, and invite their reasons for choosing it. Some large lecture halls have two central aisles, which makes legitimizing a third position both intellectually defensible and physically possible. "Those who repudiate both the hawks and the doves (or Burke and Paine) for what you think is a more reasonable position, sit in the middle." Now three groups are invited to state their positions. The dimensions of learning increase. Students in the middle, for example, might learn how difficult it is to try to remain neutral on heated emotional issues or during revolutionary times.

For those teachers willing occasionally to risk a little classroom chaos for uncertain learning outcomes (though really no less uncertain than what happens to our eloquent words in student notes during a traditional lecture), role playing and simulations are guaranteed to add energy, participation, and interaction to large lecture hall courses. I have written elsewhere (Frederick, 1981) in more detail about using simulated role playing, so here I will just sketch the outlines of this lecture variation.

There are many simulation games on contemporary issues in the social sciences, but most are too expensive and time consuming to seriously consider using in our large classes. Therefore, I prefer to create my own less elaborate games, putting students into the many roles represented in some historical event or period. The process is not as complicated as one might think. First, a minilecture establishes the context and setting for the role playing (defined as a loose simulation of actors and problems). Second, the class is divided into a number of small groups (of varying sizes and including duplicate roles depending on class size), and each group is assigned a clearly delineated role. Third, each group is given a specific, concrete task—usually to propose a position and course of action. And fourth, the proposals emanating from different groups will inevitably conflict with each other in some way—ideologically, tactically, racially, regionally, or over scarce funds, land, jobs, power, or resources.

The format of such sessions can take whatever direction a professor wishes, given careful and clear planning and directions, assertive leadership, and a lot of luck. One could hear the proposals of different groups and immediately incorporate them into a lecture on how what really happened reflected many of these same conflicts. Or, one could carry out the role-playing process longer by structuring a meeting or convention to consider the differing groups' proposals. The student groups could be instructed to prepare speeches and see the deliberations through to some conclusion, and then to caucus to develop strategies, coalitions, and tactics for achieving their goals. Neat, simple, clear closures are not easy (short of the class-ending buzzer), but this variation for large lecture classes has tremendous potential for experiential learning and, of course, involves enormous energy and interaction. Whenever the professor wishes, debriefing the exercise—which is essential—is an opportunity to restore order, to identify what was learned, and to make the transition to the next topic and pedagogical approach, probably a traditional lecture.

In conclusion: in each of these various suggestions I have sought to show that large lecture-hall classes need not be barriers to providing the kind of interactive, engaging, investigative experiences that enhance student learning. It is, I suppose, obviously easier to deliver a conventional lecture for the full fifty minutes, ending with the obligatory (and usually failing) invitation: "any questions?" Instructors should not be misled: planning and structuring active learning in large classes takes time and energy. But the rewards, both for students and instructors, are enormously satisfying. The excitement of active learning is injected into precisely the place where it is least expected. In this way instructors renew their commitment to the highest challenges of their calling. And, after using a variety of these active approaches with a large class, one might even finish a traditional lecture and ask, "Any questions?"—and be pleasantly surprised by an active response.

References

Dunham, R. E., and Gleason, M. "Challenges of the Introductory Course." In K. I. Spear (ed.), *Rejuvenating Introductory Courses.* New Directions for Teaching and Learning, no. 20. San Francisco: Jossey-Bass, 1984.

Frederick, P. "The Dreaded Discussion: Ten Ways to Start." *Improving College and University Teaching,* 1981, *29* (3), 109–114.

National Institute of Education. *Involvement in Learning: Realizing the Potential of American Higher Education.* Washington, D.C.: U.S. Department of Education, 1984.

Peter J. Frederick is professor of history and chair of the Division of Social Sciences at Wabash College.

It is passion that creates the intense, driving, transcending feeling that can raise lecturing to a special plane of greatness.

Lecturing: Essential Communication Strategies

Richard L. Weaver II, Howard W. Cotrell

How can lecturers teaching large classes of students who are inclined not to be involved fight their resistance? How can they achieve a sense of passion in the lecture hall? In this chapter we discuss essential communication strategies, such as managing instructor anxiety, using presentation time efficiently, motivating students, communicating enthusiasm, and organizing content. No set of strategies can guarantee passion because those who have a strong dislike for or lack a sense of devotion to the lecture are likely to be uninspired despite efforts to the contrary. These essential strategies, however, are likely to have significant impact. As Erickson and Erickson (1979) observe, "The large lecture class, utilizing contemporary teaching materials adapted to the expectancies of today's student, constitutes a potential learning arena where interaction, active participation, and student motivation can occur" (p. 225).

Managing Instructor Anxiety

"A lecturer's communicative patterns in the lecture hall are closely related to his or her attitudes toward self and others" (Weaver and Cotrell, 1985a). And the teaching format that generates the most apprehension has to do with public communication—lecturing. Research suggests that as

M. G. Weimer (ed.). *Teaching Large Classes Well.*
New Directions for Teaching and Learning, no. 32. San Francisco: Jossey-Bass, Winter 1987.

much as 20 percent of the adult population may experience communication apprehension (McCroskey, 1977), anxiety associated with real or anticipated communication with others. This anxiety can be strong enough to lower self-esteem and motivation. It is important to distinguish communication anxiety from stage fright, which involves specific situations such as lecturing. Stage fright is a normal experience and may or may not be accompanied by high levels of communication apprehension. Whether people have major problems interacting with others is not our concern here unless this results in nervousness when asked to present ideas in public. Thus, our comments will relate to the lecture situation only.

In another source we have suggested the process of imaging for increasing self-concept and lecturing effectiveness (Weaver and Cotrell, 1985a). Imaging is the process of creating a mental representation of a sensory or perceptual-like experience that occurs in the absence of the stimulus that would produce the genuine experience (Richardson, 1969). Lecturers must first decide on the image they want to portray in the lecture hall. For example, they may see themselves as anxiety-free, enthusiastic, and animated. If organization is a key problem, they may see themselves as well-organized and disciplined. These are outcome images because they provide the ultimate desired goals for which they are striving. Next, they must break down that outcome image into workable, achievable units. The unorganized professor might first work on a clear introduction for lectures. This is an important beginning. Then he or she may work on overall lecture structure, then on transitions between ideas, and finally on a strong conclusion that ties all the ideas together. Some writers call this *successive approximations*, where people break their eventual goal (the outcome image) into a series of subgoals (McCullough and Mann, 1985; Weaver and Cotrell, 1986). Third, lecturers need to use *systematic sensitization* (the process of building proper images incrementally) to push out negative behavior with positive activity (Weaver and Cotrell, 1985a, 1986; Ellis and Harper, 1975).

The process of imaging, sometimes including visualization, has proven to be an effective way to manage anxiety (Ayres and Hopf, 1985). Imaging is a useful activity. It can increase self-concept, cause lecturers to experiment, create a new image, and reduce apprehension. Imaging involves lecturers imagining themselves (actually seeing their selves) successfully delivering a lecture before their class. This is the outcome image. Next, they build a systematic sensitization sequence that has them accomplishing specific communication objectives (Ayres and Hopf, 1986). Any systematic sensitization sequence must be adapted to one's personal needs. A model sequence especially useful for developing successful lecturing before large classes is given in Ayres and Hopf (1985, November 1986).

There are other ways, too, to reduce anxiety. It may help lecturers to realize that those to whom they will be speaking are not only younger, but also less knowledgeable than they. In addition, understanding that those listening want and need the information the lecturer is presenting creates a positive mental set. If lecturers select ideas with which they have some familiarity, prepare lectures thoroughly, and try not to take too many unnecessary risks (such as telling jokes or digressing greatly from their prepared material), they are likely to give a satisfactory, if dull, lecture. One survey of master lecturers discovered that adequate preparation may have a direct effect in reducing anxieties related to speaking before a large audience (Lawson-Smith, 1978).

Reducing and managing anxiety can result, also, from both audio- and videotaping of lectures coupled with self-analysis, evaluation, and goal setting to assist in improvement (Phillips, 1977). Careful performance critiques are useful. For gaining constructive criticism, lecturers can seek assistance from a colleague, confidant, or from a speech-communication instructor.

Other suggestions for reducing and managing anxiety associated with lecturing are the same as those given to beginning speakers facing their early speeches. Lecturers should be at their best both physically and mentally. They should concentrate on communicating eye to eye with their students to whatever extent possible in large lecture halls. But eye-to-eye contact is not as important as the message! They should use instructional material that both creates anticipation and draws attention away from themselves.

Several other points are useful regarding anxiety. First, most students will not recognize how tense lecturers are, especially if lecturers appear confident. Second, many lecturers are their own worst critic. Their lecturing ability is not nearly as bad as they tell themselves it is. Third, some nervousness is helpful because it gives an edge and a sense of spontaneity, anticipation, excitement, and alertness. Fourth, nervousness will decrease with experience. Nervousness nurtures itself just as success does. With success will come greater successes. Fifth, for those with chronic anxiety problems, there are numerous treatment programs available (Hoffman and Sprague, 1982; Foss, 1982).

Why be concerned about managing anxiety? Anxiety can conceal passion; thus, it is important for instructors to reduce anxiety so their passion is evident to students. We are not suggesting that passion must be obvious, but anxiety should not be so intense that it is the only thing observed, thus distracting from the instructor's strong devotion to the subject.

Using Presentation Time Efficiently

Much efficiency depends on lecturer objectives. What needs to be accomplished? This may be partially determined by course goals and partially by daily class objectives. Lecturers need to carefully plan how they intend to use class time. This may depend on the role of the course in the department, whether other instructors depend on this course to provide specific kinds of background knowledge or skills, what the students are like, and what their current concerns are (McKeachie, 1986).

Some lecturers plan their class time simply by coordinating their reading assignments and examinations with their planned in-class activities. Thus, the topics discussed in class correspond to the material being read outside of class. In this way students get a well-integrated course where class activities, lectures, and readings closely parallel each other. Lecturers' actual use of presentation time, then, is carefully coordinated around in-class exercises, activities, and, perhaps, minilectures that complement and reinforce student reading. To do this successfully requires precision timing, which involves not only making sure there is enough time to get everything in but also willingness to watch the clock to make certain class time is well-spaced.

One important aspect of using lecture time effectively is variety. Certainly a major reason for dullness in lectures is lack of variety. Lecturers tend to fill their class period with information, and much of it is delivered in one style with little student feedback or interaction. Although this may be perceived as efficient by lecturers because it conveys a large amount of information with very little energy expended in delivering it, students are likely to view it as boring.

There are numerous ways to achieve variety. One is by increasing the interaction between lecturer and students. Elsewhere we have suggested a method whereby lecturers can gradually increase the amount of interaction (Weaver and Cotrell, 1986). The systematic sensitization sequence we suggest to increase student-audience participation includes seven steps: (1) rhetorical questions, (2) show of hands, (3) direct questions, (4) short surveys, (5) interaction between class members in dyads, (6) use of triads, and (7) small-group work. Notice in the sequence that it begins with instructor-student interaction and ends with student-student interaction, which is not impossible to manage, even in a big class.

Lecturers can begin by writing rhetorical questions into their lecture notes, and later asking for a show of hands to a question they ask during the lecture. At a third level they can ask a direct question, listen, and then respond to students. At another time, they might run short surveys with a showing of hands. They could encourage interaction by having students discuss a lecture point with their neighbor or in groups of three. Lecturers can have students discuss a particularly controversial point in small groups in the lecture hall. Students can be asked to discuss material they were assigned to read, develop new ideas or models, explain or discover examples for lecture material, solve problems, take examinations, or any other interesting challenge (Weaver,

1983a). Classes that include audience interaction are likely to be interesting, enjoyable, and effective.

A unique technique for gaining variety in the lecture hall is the half-sheet response (Weaver and Cotrell, 1985b). During lecture, students are asked to tear out a half-sheet of notebook paper and to put their name and the date in the upper right-hand corner. The half-sheet can be used to gain an immediate reaction to lecture material, to have students provide an example of a concept, to test student understanding, to run brief surveys, and for quizzes. Sometimes they are used for several purposes during the same lecture. Students respond to the half-sheet responses as aids to their understanding, challenges to thinking, outlets for feedback, stimulation and motivation, and reducing the anxiety of testing. The half-sheet response may also reduce lecturer anxiety by reducing the focus of the student on the lecturer alone.

It should be clear from the many alternative lecturers have for presenting material that clear, well-developed objectives are necessary. Perhaps the most efficient use of class time is the straight, stand-up, traditional lecture. But students learn better when they interact with the lecture material, the instructor, and other students (Zayas-Baya, 1977–1978; Weaver, 1974). Ways of promoting that interaction are essential to teachers of large classes, which encourage passivity.

Motivating Students

Motivation is a word used to describe the processes that arouse and stimulate student behavior, give direction and purpose to that behavior, continue to allow that behavior to persist, and lead students to choosing or preferring a particular behavior (Wlodkowski, 1982). The lecturer's first job must be to reach out and grasp students' attention. This can be accomplished in several ways, or these techniques can be combined to capture audience attention:

1. Before beginning a lecture, allow a couple of minutes of adjustment time—letting the students get wound down, reoriented, and settled. If you put your key sentence first, they are likely to miss it. You might start a lecture with some nonsensical item just to let students know that you are starting to talk: "This lecture is like all our other lectures," you might say, "it starts out slowly, then tapers off."

2. Try to get students to see where you are coming from, where you are going, what you are doing to do with their time, and how your inspirational activities relate, or eventually will relate, to them. You can do this by giving an initial forecast or brief review of major points or ideas to be developed subsequently. Then, if transitions are weak or nonexistent, or if students miss one of them, they can still interact with the lecture.

Using initial forecasting is similar to using the principle of the advanced organizer (Ausubel, 1960). Lecturers need to precede their lecture with a general and abstract statement that relates new learning to previous learning, comparing the two, and then to present the strong, obvious organizational pattern of the material that follows. New content, then, needs to be arranged in coherent subpassages of two or three minutes duration (West, 1968).

3. If you can begin with a story, an example, a startling statistic, a personal experience, or something that has significant attention-holding appeal, attention will be captured. Sometimes it helps to know that this is the kind of lecture-opening material one should collect. Lectures are similar to chess games: they have opening, middle, and ending strategies. Effective lecturers are constantly on the lookout for a variety of strategies they can use.

But in all of this, too, it is important to know that attention does not last long. It is fleeting. Thus, do not think about holding attention just at the outset of the lecture; holding attention is important throughout the lecture. Lecturers hold attention throughout a lecture by using techniques that captivate imagination.

What can lecturers do to maintain student interest? Several things are very effective:

1. Adapt your lecture material to your students. Share information with them that concerns them. Share information with them that they can handle. Try not to get needlessly esoteric or theoretical if the students cannot handle it or if the material does not merit it. Analyze your student audience first to find out where they are.

2. Do not try to pack your whole educational career—all that you have learned—into the lecture or course.

3. It is better to cover a few points or topics in-depth than many points or topics superficially. Do not think you have to cover the entire discipline. Narrowing the focus will help hold students' interest. Consider, too, they can only remember so much.

4. Interest also comes from variety. Most speakers know that a long string of statistics, a series of historical anecdotes, or a long list of facts does not hold attention well. Variety of material captures attention. As a lecturer, try to assemble facts as well as examples, opinions as well as illustrations, statistics as well as anecdotes. Even a good storyteller can bore an audience if his or her repertoire includes just one story after another with no other intervening material. We suspect that durable learning probably occurs more in the form of spontaneous combustion than as a response to methodical coercion. Capitalize, if you can, on ideas that are generated at the moment—products of that particular unique circumstance.

5. Variety also results from format. Try to vary your lecturing for-

mat. Do not just talk to students. Strive for give-and-take whenever possible. Move around. Do not stand in one place. Lecturing does not mean the lecturer and lectern are one. Use visual materials—the chalkboard, charts, graphs, maps, pictures, books, magazines. This forces movement, and as one student summarized it well, "I'd rather see a lecture than hear one." Use films, slides, the overhead projector, or television.

6. Be aware that motivation also comes from the use of humor. To use humor does not require that a classroom instructor be a wit, kidder, gag man, punster, or clown. Rather, humor emanates from the subject matter and setting. This gives the lecturer control over the kind and extent of the humor in the classroom. Not only that, it opens up humorous possibilities for all instructors.

Humor can build the lecturer-student relationship. It can help break the ice, reduce fear, encourage a sense of trust, and establish a feeling of camaraderie and of mutuality, all too often missing in a large class setting. Humor sets the tone for a more relaxed atmosphere (Robinson, 1977). It may offer lecturers a way to introduce a topic, a lecture, or a course. Because of its play frame, it can provide a vehicle for moving in and out of serious situations (Robinson, 1977, p. 41). In using humor, a framework needs to be established that is recognized by all concerned. Writing on humor, Eastman said, "The first law of humor is that things can be funny only when we are in fun" (1948, p. 3).

Students learn best in an environment where they are somewhat comfortable, but especially where they enjoy the situation. Enjoyment can be encouraged through the use of humor. It is contagious; thus, if lecturers enjoy what they are doing, it is more likely that students will also enjoy the situation.

Communicating Enthusiasm

The first generation of students raised on "Sesame Street"' are now in college. The potential effect of this bears directly on lecturer enthusiasm. Sesame Street conveys short bursts of information in a manner that is full of action, is entertaining, and is sometimes surprising. Lecturers may not be able to fully compete with this format; however, they need not resign themselves to failure either. Failure means more of the same for students: lectures that are boring, uninteresting, passive, and uninvolving (Weaver, 1983b). Lecturers need to strive to model enthusiasm.

Eleanor Roosevelt said, "If teachers can accumulate degrees and write books, well and good, but the first requisite should be their ability to inspire youth." If there is one instructor characteristic related to learning, it is enthusiasm (Coats and Smidchens, 1966; Isaacson, McKeachie, and Milholland, 1963; Weaver, 1982). Enthusiasm is the most convincing orator. It is like an infallible law of nature. The simplest person, fired with enthusiasm, is more persuasive than the most eloquent person without it. There is no question that those lecturers who demonstrate dynamism in their presentations have less difficult holding student attention, especially in large classes. Lecturers need a certain amount of aggressiveness, boldness, and forcefulness. They can do this by:

1. Demonstrating an active commitment to the topic, by showing what they have done, how they are involved, and what their plans are for future involvement.

2. Demonstrating an emotional commitment—complete ego involvement. Instructors can let students know that they believe in what they are doing, that your knowledge, ideas, and information can make a difference—by being a believer!

3. Being intellectually and physically powerful. Instructors should try to eliminate speech hesitancies such as "uh," "er," "you know," "I mean," and "okay."

Students' comments on what motivates them leave no doubt. The following comments come from students we questioned about motivation in an interpersonal communication class in 1986. One said, "I get motivated by an instructor who enjoys what he or she is teaching." Another said, "The enthusiasm presented by the lecturer is the best motivator," and still another said, "Energetic professors—who not only have a great deal of knowledge, but truly want to share their knowledge and will go out of their way to enable students to learn from them are what motivates me the most." Enthusiasm is contagious. One student explained it this way: "In a class where the teacher just stands there and talks in a monotone with no enthusiasm, I get extremely bored. I figure, if the teacher doesn't care any more than that, why should I?" Another said, "I derive my energy for learning from his or her zest for the material. . . ." If enthusiasm is the yeast that makes your hopes rise, then it applies to lecturers as well as to students, and lecturers need to realize that such enthuasiam in students often can be directly lecturer inspired.

Some lecturers become so task-oriented, so content-bound, so procedure-driven, that they lose sight of the students they are instructing. Passion is dead. When everything is so tightly scheduled, for example, that there is no freedom to be spontaneous, caring suffers. We know one instructor who conducts each class in exactly this manner. Students enter, take assigned seats, copy the homework assignment from the chalkboard while attendance is taken. The forty-five minute lesson follows exactly prepared objectives. Students take notes, often take a quiz, and know exactly how to prepare for the next day. Instructor and students are prepared; there is no guesswork, no floundering in the classroom. But does this exactness and preparation reflect that the instructor really cares about students? Even lecturing can be one-to-one when students feel lecturers care just about them. A form of immediacy—even urgency—can occur even in large classes.

Lecturers need to appear as fallible, responsive, human beings capable of transcending their mistakes. They need to be human in front of their students. The behaviors of lecturers before students need to be as close to the day-to-day actions and reactions as that of normal, alert, responsive individuals. These are the models students can emulate. Can instructors accept students' ideas? Can they develop students' ideas? Can they accept and develop students' feelings? Can they give students freedom and praise rather than criticism; can they encourage, listen, allow for student talk in the back rows, accept student mistakes, make their own mistakes, and appear authentic?

Those instructors who wear their elitist professional roles at all times in front of students, who hold students at a distance, and who are unwilling to be real—themselves—in front of their students, do a disservice. The time to be real, to be one's authentic self, to reveal the passion one has for teaching students zest for life, to demonstrate one's wholeness and individuality, is in the lecture hall. When students can view lecturers as individuals with thoughts, feelings, values, and beliefs, then the lecturers break through the artificial barriers and show, in the best sense of the word, lecturer enthusiasm. Students like lecturers who are warm, considerate, cheerful, and friendly. Lowman observed that lecturers "who are excited by their subject, caught up in the fascination of what they teach, foster student enthusiasm for the subject by personal example" (1984, p. 183). Ralph Waldo Emerson said, "Nothing great was ever achieved without enthusiasm," and that applies to impassioned teaching as much as to anything.

Organizing Content

Traditional approaches to lecturing require traditional organization schemes. Lecturers may provide the outline of their lecture for students at the outset, carefully follow that outline throughout the lecture, then summarize each main point at the end. Although some students may be pleased to get this much organization from some of the lecturers, this format, too, can become repetitious and dull.

To get excitement, add interest, and discover new methods for organizing their content, lecturers need to break out of their "traditional" rut—not that it isn't appropriate for some topics. There are a variety of ways to do this and still maintain a lecture orientation. One writer suggests dividing the lecture into segments of time where the students just listen to the lecture and a time when they write down what they have heard (Bentley, 1981). Other writers suggest periodically dividing the students into small groups to discuss the material, thus, encouraging more active student participation in the lecture (Bowman, 1979; Kelly and Holmes, 1979; Napell, 1978; Stanton, 1978; Weaver, 1983a). Developing a series of questions that help to frame a concept or subject is another approach to modifying the lecture method (Osterman and Coffey, 1980). Another writer recommends having students summarize either orally or in writing during planned pauses (West, 1968). Still another approach is the use of games (Thiagarajan, 1978). This by no means exhausts the suggestions made for changing the lecture presentation format (Weaver and Michel, 1982). Lecturers need to investigate methods to change their organization and approach to provide students with appealing lecture experiences.

In one of our classes we try to make certain that no one day looks exactly like any other. We may begin by sharing some half-sheet responses from the previous lecture. We may have a quiz on the reading assignment next, or we may put this at the end of the lecture. We often have a mini-lecture that relates to the topic in the readings. Sometimes we have a survey or a series of survey questions—some of these generated by the students during the last class period. We like to encourage dyadic work, so we may offer students a challenge that needs to be confronted or resolved. Also, we like to give students an opportunity to relate material to their own lives and problems, so we may have them, at some point, respond to a question that is germane not only to the study material, but also, possibly, to their personal lives. Often, we have a short editorial-length piece from some writer who has an insight on the problem or topic at hand. How these pieces get organized may have to do with how they relate to each other, the pace of the class, the restlessness or receptivity of the students, or how we feel on that day. We list the things we want to accomplish on an 8½-inch by 11-inch pad of paper. We may not follow the order they are arranged in, but we might. On some days, we may not accomplish all that we set out to, and things left over are either dropped or carried to the next class period. We have learned that students tend to like closure; thus, we try not to begin a lecture or activity that will need to carry over to the next class period. Much is left to spontaneity—how we feel about or sense what is happening.

The main point of our approach to each lecture is that we like variety. We are always looking for pieces to work with. With many pieces (much like a puzzle), we can assemble them in any order that seems right at the time. One order may well be better than another, and after a class we may write ourselves notes for the next time we use these pieces: "Be sure to follow this activity with the quotation," "This exercise took too long; needs to be shortened," or "Do the quiz first and get it out of the way." We may even number the parts that were used so that we can follow the exact order the next time. This process of fitting pieces to learing experiences is what makes teaching a challenging, exciting, spontaneous experience—as much fun for the lecturer as for the students.

Whatever methods lecturers select, however, should follow several important organizing principles. First, any approach must satisfy the lecturer's learning objectives. In this way—by identifying the learning objectives first—lecturers can make certain material has not become too abstract or irrelevant. Second, lecturers should have a single theme, or at least, a number of subjects related by an overriding concept or topic. Thematic unity helps to unify the approach and aids student understanding. Third, lecturers should reveal simplicity of subject matter. In a survey of essential qualities of master lecturers, one researcher discovered that the common characteristics were simplicity of subject matter and the abundant use of examples (Davis, 1965). If lecturers could follow these principles alone, lectures would surely improve. To follow such principles requires diligence, concern, and commitment—passion.

Conclusion

What is the ideal picture of lecturers with large audiences? People in front of audiences who are both sensitive and responsive to the enthusiastic synergy and excitement in their listeners. They provide listeners with means for launching themselves on new adventures in learning, alternatives for moving themselves off dead center when they have reached learning plateaus, and opportunities for overcoming the war weariness that is frequently occasioned in the battle for learning (Thompson, 1974).

Accomplishing this motivational task may be beyond the resources of many lecturers. But it need not be. There are specific communication strategies lecturers can use to attain this goal. Anxiety can be managed if understood and approached systematically. Presentation time can be used efficiently if lecturers seek variety by increasing lecturer-student interaction, using the half-sheet response and other methods designed specifically to involve students. Lecturers must unleash students' self-motivation in the beginning and throughout the lecture. Enthusiasm can be the result if lecturers reduce their task orientation and begin to appear flexible, responsive, and capable of making mistakes. Lecturers need to be warm, considerate, cheerful, and friendly. To break out of their traditional lecturing mode, lecturers need to investigate methods to change their approach while keeping in mind the basic principles of satisfying learning objectives, maintaining a unifying theme, and achieving simplicity.

What do lecturers really want? When people really want something, they go after it with passion. Passion may be precisely the element missing from lecturing. Realistically, effective lecturing is not within the grasp of every teacher. The communication strategies discussed here require dedication and commitment. But that may be insufficient. It is passion that creates the intense, driving, transcending feeling that can raise lecturing to its special plane of greatness. And passion cannot be taught. It is the key to effective learning and to command of the essential communication strategies.

68

References

Ausubel, D. P. "The Use of Advanced Organizers in the Learning and Retention of Meaningful Verbal Material." *Journal of Educational Psychology*, 1960, *51*, 267–272.

Ayres, J., and Hopf, T. S. "Visualization: A Means of Reducing Speech Anxiety." *Communication Education*, 1985, *34*, 318–323.

Ayres, J., and Hopf, T. S. "Visualization, Systematic Desensitization, and Rational Emotive Therapy: A Comparative Evaluation." Paper presented at the Speech Communication Association, Chicago, November 1986.

Bentley, D. A. "More Ammunition for the Note-Taking Feud: 'The Spaced Lecture.'" *Improving College and University Teaching*, 1981, *29*, 85–87.

Bowman, J. S. "The Lecture-Discussion Format Revisited." *Improving College and University Teaching*, 1979, *27*, 25–27.

Coats, W. D., and Smidchens, U. "Audience Recall as a Function of Speaker Dynamism." *Journal of Educational Psychology*, 1966, *57*, 189–191.

Davis, R. J. "Secrets of Master Lecturers." *Improving College and University Teaching*, 1965, *13*, 150–151.

Eastman, M. *Enjoyment of Laughter*. New York: Simon & Schuster, 1948.

Ellis, A., and Harper, R. A. *A New Guide to Rational Living*. North Hollywood, Calif.: Melvin Powers Wilshire Book, 1975.

Erickson, K. V., and Erickson, M. T. "Simulation and Game Exercises in Large Lecture Classes." *Communication Education*, 1979, *28*, 224–229.

Foss, K. A. "Communication Apprehension: Resources for the Instructor." *Communication Education*, 1982, *31*, 195–203.

Hoffman, J., and Sprague, J. "A Survey of Reticence and Communication Apprehension Treatment Programs at U.S. Colleges and Universities." *Communication Education*, 1982, *31*, 185–193.

Isaacson, R. L., McKeachie, W. J., and Milholland, J. E. "Correlation of Teacher Personality Variables and Student Ratings." *Journal of Educational Psychology*, 1963, *54*, 110–117.

Kelly, B. W., and Holmes, J. "The Guided Lecture Procedure." *Journal of Reading*, 1979, *22*, 602–604.

Lawson-Smith, C. *The Lecture: A Vital Component of University Life: A Guide to Assist Faculty*. Montreal: Office of Educational Development, McGill University, 1978. ED 202 256

Lowman, J. *Mastering the Techniques of Teaching*. San Francisco: Jossey-Bass, 1984.

McCroskey, J. C. "Oral Communication Apprehension: A Summary of Recent Theory and Research." *Human Communication Research*, 1977, *4*, 78–96.

McCullough, C. J., and Mann, R. W. *Managing Your Anxiety: Regaining Control When You Feel Stressed, Helpless, and Alone*. Los Angeles: Jeremy P. Tarcher, 1985.

McKeachie, W. J. *Teaching Tips: A Guidebook for the Beginning College Teacher*. 8th ed. Lexington, Mass.: Heath, 1986.

Napell, S. M. "Updating the Lecture." *Journal of Teacher Education*, 1978, *29*, 53–56.

Osterman, D. N., and Coffey, B. *A New Teaching Approach: The Feedback Lecture*. Corvallis: Oregon State University, 1980. ED 190 121

Phillips, G. M. "Rhetoritherapy Versus the Medical Model: Dealing with Reticence." *Communication Education*, 1977, *26*, 34–43.

Richardson, A. *Mental Imagery*. London: Routledge and Kegan Paul, 1969.

Robinson, V. M. *Humor in the Health Professions.* Thorofare, N.J.: Charles B. Slack, 1977.

Stanton, H. E. "Small Group Teaching in the Lecture Situation." *Improving College and University Teaching,* 1978, *26,* 69–70.

Thiagarajan, S. *How to Use Frame Games to Unlecture Your Teaching.* Bloomington, Ind.: IA Publications, 1978.

Thompson, R. "Legitimate Lecturing." *Improving College and University Teaching,* 1974, *22,* 163–164.

Weaver, R. L., II. "The Use of Exercises and Games." *The Speech Teacher,* 1974, *23,* 302–311.

Weaver, R. L., II. "Positive Qualities of the Large Group Lecturer." *Focus on Learning,* 1982, *8,* 10–13.

Weaver, R. L., II. "The Small Group in Large Classes." *The Educational Forum,* 1983a, *48,* 65–73.

Weaver, R. L., II. *Understanding Public Communication.* Englewood Cliffs, N.J.: Prentice-Hall, 1983b.

Weaver, R. L., II, and Cotrell, H. W. "Imaging Can Increase Self-Concept and Lecturing Effectiveness." *Education,* 1985a, *105,* 264–270.

Weaver, R. L., II, and Cotrell, H. W. "Mental Aerobics: The Half-Sheet Response." *Innovative Higher Education,* 1985b, *10,* 23–31.

Weaver, R. L., II, and Cotrell, H. W. "Using Interactive Images in the Lecture Hall." *Educational Horizons,* 1986, *64,* 180–185.

Weaver, R. L., II, and Michel, T. A. *On Lecturing: A Selected Bibliography.* Bowling Green, Ohio: School of Speech Communication, Bowling Green State University, 1982. ED 225 217

West, C. K. "The Modified Lecture: A Useful Technique for the Teacher." *Clearing House,* 1968, *42,* 142–144.

Wlodkowski, R. J. *Motivation* (Rev. ed.) Washington, D.C.: National Education Association, 1982.

Zayas-Baya, E. P. "Instructional Media in the Total Language Picture." *International Journal of Instructional Media,* 1977–78, *5,* 145–150.

Richard L. Weaver II is professor in the Department of Interpersonal and Public Communication at Bowling Green State University. He directs the basic speech communication course that enrolls more than two thousand students per year.

Howard W. Cotrell is associate professor in the Instructional Media Center at Bowling Green State University. He and Dr. Weaver have written a number of articles in the area of instructional communication.

Evaluation need not be a dreaded but necessary evil.
Experienced instructors have learned how to modify evaluation
and feedback methods in large classes to reduce their negative
qualities and improve student motivation and achievement.

Giving Students Feedback

Joseph Lowman

> *Testing and grading form one corner of the learning*
> *pyramid, but for entirely too long both have been considered*
> *independent of learning.*
> —Milton, Pollio, and Eisen, 1986, p. 201

Giving students feedback sounds simple enough: instructors assign work, evaluate students' performance, and tell them how well they did. In reality, evaluation and feedback are as complex, replete with pitfalls for the uninitiated, and important to student and instructor satisfaction as any other single topic related to teaching the large class. Few topics have as much to do with what students learn as the procedures for evaluating student performance and giving feedback on it.

Evaluation issues are critical in any college class. Students' satisfaction with well-thought-out and delivered lectures and their motivation to do what teachers ask of them can easily be eclipsed by evaluation methods they see as vague, arbitrary, trivial, or—worst of all—unfair. Evaluation is the single most important topic to the interpersonal rapport of a college class (Lowman, 1984).

The problems and challenges of evaluating students are magnified as a direct result of the increased number of students in a large class (McGee, 1986). Because secretaries require more lead time to prepare large numbers of examinations, instructors must construct their examinations

M. G. Weimer (ed.). *Teaching Large Classes Well.*
New Directions for Teaching and Learning, no. 32. San Francisco: Jossey-Bass, Winter 1987.

farther in advance. An instructor of a class of fifty who can tolerate three students calling up to beg off the next day's exam will find it hard to receive with good humor the thirty such requests that can be expected in a class of five hundred. Transporting 250 or more test booklets from the professor's office to the classroom where the test is to be given can require both strength and endurance. The ordinarily simple job of handing out exams to students can easily consume the first fifteen minutes of a fifty-minute test period if tests are passed down rows of waiting students. Even more time consuming are the tasks of grading examinations, recording the grades, and returning them to students. Because of the practical problems that are related to class size, "The large class reduces the teacher's sense of freedom in choosing teaching methods, assigning papers, or testing to achieve varying objectives" (McKeachie, 1978, p. 207).

Interpersonal problems also increase as a function of size. A heightened sense of personal distance will be felt by students and instructors alike in the large class. Such distance is likely to promote the unfortunate behaviors of skipping class, arriving late, talking to classmates, leaving early, putting off studying until the last moment, or cheating. Increased interpersonal distance may make many instructors more likely to over-emphasize evaluation or to treat it in an overly rigid manner, to evaluate student work more harshly, to adopt more intrusive police policies to catch students who may be cheating, or to be less concerned about individual students whose performance is poor. Diffusion of individual responsibility occurs in all groups as size increases (Shaw and Costanzo, 1982), with unfortunate consequences in large classes, as both students and teachers become more likely to treat one another as faceless stereotypes than as distinct individuals.

Evaluation need not be a dreaded necessary evil in the large class, however. Experienced instructors have learned how to modify methods to evaluate and give feedback so as to reduce their negative qualities and to improve student motivation and achievement. This chapter will discuss some of the special challenges of evaluation in the large class and will present some solutions to common problems. Underlying the specific suggestions is an optimistic attitude about the important role of evaluation and feedback in promoting learning, applicable to classes of any size.

Evaluation Issues in All College Classrooms

College classrooms are rich interpersonal arenas where students show the same kinds of emotional reactions (many of them subtle and symbolic) to their instructors as employees show to their supervisors (Lowman, 1984). An instructor's style of motivating students interacts with differences in their abilities and personalities and influences how hard they work outside of class and, consequently, how much they learn. How students' work is evaluated, however, has more to do with what they learn than simply how motivated they are to work.

Milton, Pollio, and Eisen (1986) argue that teaching, testing, and learning cannot be separated and that many evils of American higher education result from the view that they are independent. Among the myths about college grades that these authors cite are the following:

- Grades from one class or school can be taken out of context and compared to grades given elsewhere ("He's a solid B student.")
- The apparent metric precision of differences in grade point averages (GPAs) is meaningful given that the GPA is based on a few crude categories ("If I make an A in this class I can graduate with a 2.875.")
- The major effect of college tests and grades is to increase learning ("I wouldn't learn anything in a course if I didn't have the test to make me study.").

To Milton and his colleagues, grades are subjective, imprecise, and used more to promote conformity and to select students for graduate or professional schools than to promoting learning, which their research indicates instructors, parents, even students indicate should be the major purpose of evaluation.

Viewing college grades from an interpersonal perspective, especially seeing the analogy between classrooms and work settings, suggests ways to use evaluation to promote learning. Just as some workers are motivated mostly by external rewards, some students—those with what Eisen (1981) calls a Grade Orientation (GO)—are motivated primarily by the external reward of grades. GO students see the classroom mainly as a stressful setting in which they will be tried and tested. As noted in Milton, Pollio, and Eisen (1986), "students who are highly motivated by grades tend to be more concerned about what impression they create on their instructor than with learning the content of lectures" (p. 175).

In contrast, in the work setting, some workers seem more motivated to seek their own sources of satisfaction than just the boss's approval or the pay check. Similarly, students with a Learning Orientation (LO) view the classroom more as an opportunity for personal satisfaction than as a crucible. For LO students a college course represents not only a series of challenges to be met, but also a context in which to encounter significant new information and ideas.

Instructors can easily place too much emphasis on the external rewards of grades and unintentionally encourage a GO in students, making it less likely they will grow toward a LO, something that is seen more commonly in seniors than freshmen. The following are ways instructors may encourage a GO (adapted from a list in Milton, Pollio, and Eisen, 1986).

- Use frequent tests (possibly surprise tests) to reward students who have done the assigned reading and to punish those who have not
- Communicate the expectation that students will not attend class regularly except to get notes on material that will be on the exams
- Penalize students who are absent from class or who turn in assignments late by reducing the grades their work is given
- Post test grades as the sole means of giving feedback or return answer sheets or test booklets that do not allow a student to see what were the correct answers to the questions that were missed.
- Assume some grading credit, however trivial, must be given to any student who elects to do outside reading, writing, or participation in research projects and rarely assign non-graded work.

Though difficult to accomplish with many students long accustomed to educational practices that promote a grading orientation, instructors can encourage a learning orientation in students. This can be accomplished by avoiding the preceding practices and communicating, whenever possible, the expectation that students will want to learn material or do work for its own sake, not just for points toward their grade.

College instructors of any size course are more likely to have fewer complaints about their evaluation methods and to encourage a LO in their students if they will do the following.

- Think of your students as employees and yourself as a supervisor with the important job of motivating them to want to work independently of your direction and evaluation
- See testing as a way students can show you how much they have learned about important concepts and findings, not as a way you can find out which trivial details they have failed to pick up
- Recognize that the methods you use to evaluate your students will tell them much more about what you value and wish them to learn than what you think you are communicating to them verbally
- Notice the language you use when making assignments and discussing tests; words such as "I am requiring" and "you should" convey a more authoritarian style of leadership than the alternatives, "I would like" and "you may find"
- Remember that evaluation is only a one-way street whose purpose is to rank students according to your external standards unless you also give the kind of information that students can use for their own development
- A learning orientation can best be promoted by using evaluation techniques that reinforce students for independent learning and that give them as much specific feedback during the term as possible.

Evaluation that Promotes a Learning Orientation
in Large Classes

Large classes place pressures on instructors that can easily lead them to treat evaluation in a more mechanical and impersonal way than they might otherwise. An instructor who prefers short-answer and essay exams may resort in a large class to sole use of multiple-choice exams or, worse, to an uncritical use of items from text publishers' questions lists. Even an instructor accustomed to the use of multiple-choice exams may become less careful in their construction, scoring, and evaluation. This is not to say that most instructors of large classes are sloppy or uncaring about evaluation, just that anxiety about how to evaluate so many students may lead many to take time-saving short cuts or to assume there are no options to impersonal and mechanically applied evaluation techniques.

Pressures from having many students may also have the unfortunate consequences of making some instructors less caring about individual students than usual or more likely to adopt arbitrary policies about missed exams or deadline extensions. Worst of all is a fatalistic attitude about failing students that can be encouraged in large classes. I once heard an instructor comment, "I can't let myself get too concerned about students who are failing in my big section—there are just too many of them for me to do anything about except assign the grades they deserve."

Pressures associated with sheer numbers of students notwithstanding, instructors need not abdicate control over their evaluation techniques or preferred ways of relating to students in a large class. To reduce the liabilities of evaluation in a large class, even eliminate them altogether, instructors should seek creative solutions to the problems. The following sections discuss general considerations and specific solutions to evaluation problems in a large class. Before these are offered, a few caveats are in order.

The specific suggestions given here have been reported to be helpful, either in the teaching literature or in personal communications from college teachers during teaching workshops I have conducted around the country. Though they will help reduce the conflict between an instructor's educational objectives and the practical problems of grading large numbers of papers, they will not eliminate it. In addition, there is no guarantee these techniques will have the same positive effect for you that others report in the context of their courses. Evaluation techniques are intimately connected to an instructor's educational objectives, speaking skill, and the interpersonal climate of the classroom group. Successful evaluation is most likely to occur in classes that are successful in other ways as well.

Evaluate Your Purposes. Few college teachers will endorse encouraging a GO rather than a LO in their students. (Few students are likely to admit to preferring their orientation as well.) Yet, like everyone else, students and instructors can easily delude themselves about inconsistencies between their stated values and behavior. For example, in a study of grading practices, seventeen instructors of varied subjects reported that 31 percent of their test questions tapped complex, cognitive skills such as problem solving. Judges' ratings of their examination items, however, indicated that only 8.5 percent required complex thinking skills. Most were assessing only recall of course content (Semb and Spencer, 1976, as cited in Milton, Pollio, and Eisen, 1986). To avoid self-deception, one should evaluate one's grading practices with an especially critical eye and perhaps through the eyes of a colleague as well.

In planning the evaluation methods to be used in a large class, first ask yourself which of Bloom's (1956) learning objectives you wish to pursue and what is their relative importance in the course you will be teaching. Do you believe it is more important for your students to master the facts and theories in your course, to be able to apply course concepts to examples, or to be able to critically contrast and evaluate different concepts? (See Furhman and Grasha, 1983, p. 170, for an excellent description of Bloom's classic taxonomy.) Also, ask yourself what your methods would suggest about your implicit purposes to someone from a distant planet. For example, if your essay questions require considerable reading skill just to understand what is being sought, your actual purpose may be to assess reading skill. Similarly, if your multiple-choice items require students to perform mental gymnastics like those on intelligence tests, your exam may test academic aptitude rather than achievement. If you ask trick questions or questions that require students to remember obscure details, your actual purpose is to promote attention to and memorization of details rather than to guide students' study and evaluation of content. Asking difficult questions about very specific information that will produce a wide distribution of scores is easy. Asking difficult questions about important concepts, after making it clear that students are expected to learn them well, is more difficult, but also more appropriate.

Before deciding on the specific evaluation methods you wish to use, consider your general attitudes about college grades as well as your specific educational objectives. Do you support college grades as socially useful because they provide entry to more responsible jobs for brighter and more persevering individuals? Or, do you believe that grades should reflect only the mastery of learning objectives that are clearly spelled out in advance and are obtainable by every student? Whatever your position communicate your learning objectives to your students at the beginning of your course, showing how your evaluation methods are consistent with what you hope to accomplish.

Recognize Differences in What Students Prefer. Regardless of the specific methods you choose, you will not please everyone. Even though college teachers of all subjects give objective more often than essay tests (Lunneborg, 1977), student preferences for different kinds of evaluation techniques vary. Most students prefer multiple-choice exams when given the option of other evaluation procedures (Baker and Behrens, 1971) but some will always prefer short-answer or essay tests. Evidence reported over a number of years indicates that students study differently for various kinds of exams: multiple-choice or short-answer exams tend to promote memorization of details, essay exams promote critical evaluation and broad integration (see Lowman, 1984, and Milton, Pollio, and Eisen, 1986). Each of these findings suggests that a variety of techniques is superior to any single method. Use varied methods as much as possible to increase the likelihood of students' finding preferred ways to show what they have learned and that their preparation will be comprehensive.

General Suggestions for All Evaluation Methods

Seek Clarity. The most common student complaint about exams is that they are unclear. College teachers typically construct tests alone and items that are vague or confusing can easily slip into exams. Unless students complain about specific items—and we take their complaints seriously—we may never realize how confusing some examination items are to many students. Actively encouraging students to give teachers specific feedback about exams will make teachers more aware of their exams' limitations.

There are several ways to solicit feedback on clarity. When constructing an exam and before the final copies are typed, show a few sample items (five or so) to someone else to critique. Have the individuals (they might be colleagues who ask you to perform a similar service for them, students who have taken your courses in previous semesters, or volunteers from your present classes) complete the items in your presence—individually or in a small group—and think out loud as they answer each question. An alternative is to invite student volunteers to meet with you immediately after an exam to go over a few items in a similar way, especially the items the students found most troublesome. Stress to students that the goal of such test shaping meetings is to give you specific feedback to improve your tests in the future. In the less personal setting of the large class, active seeking of feedback on test clarity is especially needed.

Reduce the Stress of Test Administration. The practical problems associated with test administration in large classes are certain to be more stressful for students (and instructors) than in smaller courses. Much more time is required to distribute and collect exams in a class of several hundred and many more special problems will arise. Students' heightened anxiety also makes them resentful of an instructor who does not show up on test days and delegates this duty to underlings. Unless instructors administer the tests themselves and actively plan for the logistical challenges associated with test administration in a large class, test days are likely to be unnecessarily stressful for students.

A method of test administration that has worked well for me is to inform students I will be arriving ten minutes early on exam days to pass out papers, as soon as the previous class leaves the classroom. I hand students examinations as they file into the room, making it clear that they should not enter the room if they wish to do last-minute studying. Two or three people can pass out several hundred exams in this way easily and efficiently and everyone will be able to begin work by the start of the class hour. Not only does this method save students time, it also reassures them. You are there and in charge.

A similar technique can be used when you collect exams afterward. Station yourself well outside the classroom to receive papers as students leave. This keeps the associated noise and confusion from disturbing students still working and gives you a chance to chat briefly with some of them about the test. Some students will take the opportunity of inspecting an answer key or model paper before they leave if you have one available.

Give as Much Feedback as Possible. No aspect of the large class is as demanding of instructors' time or as likely to pressure them to adopt impersonal GO evaluation methods as are the challenges of grading and giving feedback. Simple arithmetic demonstrates the case. If an instructor requires about eight hours to grade a short-answer exam given to a class of fifty students, forty-eight hours will be required to grade the same exam for a class of three hundred. When it comes to grading there is almost always a conflict between educational objectives and practical considerations.

Using teaching assistants (TAs) to grade papers is for most instructors the most common solution to grading pressures in a large class. TAs create new problems, however. The task of grading papers cannot simply be assigned to TAs and forgotten. TAs require training and supervision if they are to grade papers accurately and consistently and to give specific feedback up to your standards. Even when two or three TAs are available, the primary instructor should also help with the grading to model the desired standards for the TAs and evaluate the students' performance and the exam's effectiveness firsthand.

Students are understandably disappointed and angered when an exam or paper is returned to them with only a number score or letter grade written on it. Even worse is the practice of returning only machine-scorable answer sheets to avoid constructing additional test forms. Even when students are pleased with the grades they received, they usually feel let down, even cheated, when the instructor tells them little about what they did well. Students who do poorly may have little idea of how to improve their future performance without guidance. Personal comments on papers (such as, "Good work, Karin," or "Nice improvement, Andy") are especially valued in large classes, where impersonality is the rule. Regardless of the specific evaluation methods used or the time grading may take from the instructor's schedule, students' work should be graded and returned with at least a few short personal comments scribbled somewhere on the pages. Making copies of model or exemplary student papers available for students who wish to see them also provides helpful guidance. As much as anything else, feedback with a personal touch will help to minimize the drawbacks of evaluation in a large class.

Guard Against Errors in Record Keeping. Be pessimistic when handling large numbers of papers. If you assume that something will go wrong and make backup copies of student grades, errors that may affect a student's final grade are less likely to occur. If you are comfortable using them, computers can help protect against errors, but only if you make multiple backup files and printed copies of your records and double check a sample of computer-calculated scores. A computer is far less likely to make an error than a TA or instructor in computing final averages. Above all, be exceedingly careful with student records in large classes. Your personal memory cannot be counted on to help protect students from the clerical errors that are more likely to occur.

Return Exams Efficiently and with Respect. The practical problem of matching several hundred graded papers with individual students can increase the anxiety many students experience at the moment of truth when their exams are returned. Calling out each student's name individually is obviously out of the question. It is worth thinking creatively about how to overcome this problem rather than assuming papers cannot be returned in a personal way in a large class. One solution is to have two or three individuals (student volunteers if TAs are not available) take stacks of alphabetized papers to the far corners of the room, front and rear. Announce to the class which corners have which letters of the alphabet and ask them to gather around the appropriate person. Instruct each distribution assistant to call out students' names from their papers and to return each paper personally. Several hundred exams can be returned in ten to fifteen minutes using this method in a much more efficient and respectful way than asking students to hunt for their papers through what soon become disorganized piles on the floor. Whatever other procedures you think of to handle this small but important problem, try to spread students out physically rather than concentrating them in one or two crowded spots.

Regardless of the specific evaluation methods chosen, consider first your objectives and implicit purposes and be certain your students know what these are; select varied methods that are as efficient as possible without being overly mechanical or rigid; actively seek feedback from students about your assessment procedures; and return papers with as much specific feedback and respect as possible. The next section discusses many common evaluation methods that can be modified for large sections.

Common In-Class Methods of Evaluation in Large Classes

With foresight and planning almost any method, including essays, can be used at least occasionally in large classes. However, instructors will always be faced with the problem of balancing a method's ability to promote desired learning with its ability to be graded relatively easily.

Multiple-Choice Exams. A great deal has been written about multiple-choice exams and how to construct items for them (see Lowman, 1984, and Haladyna and Downing, 1984, for summaries of this literature). What is most important to stress about effective multiple-choice tests is that just because the correct answers are predetermined and they can be scored by a computer does *not* make them objective, clear, or fair. Further, the illusion of objectivity or precision in multiple-choice exams opens instructors to the danger of assuming the test must be a good one because the distribution of scores is nicely shaped—something that will usually happen when you collect measurements of almost anything from a large group of individuals.

In effective multiple-choice exams, the following are more likely to be true:

- The instructor has a single clear idea about what point is being addressed by each item
- As a group, the items are aimed at a balanced mixture of information recall, application to examples, and contrasts among concepts
- Items are kept as simple and short as possible, especially the specific choices
- The instructor has taken the items personally (or given them to someone else) to identify unclear items beforehand
- The instructor uses an item-analysis computer program after each exam to identify overly difficult, easy, or confusing items that should be avoided next time
- Fewer items are given than in a smaller course (less actual working time and a greater range of student abilities are common in a large section)
- At least one short-answer question requiring writing is included on each exam.

Using multiple-choice exams in this way takes advantage of their ease of scoring but still allows students an opportunity, however limited, to express themselves more freely.

Short Answers, IDs, and Reverse IDs. Though exclusive use of essay exams is unlikely to be practical in any large class, short-answer or identification questions (IDs) can be used frequently, even exclusively, if an instructor is willing to construct model answers others can use to help with the grading. One or two short-answer questions can be added easily to enrich any multiple-choice exam.

The large class lends itself very well to reverse identification questions. To use this approach distribute a list of key terms or concepts to your students beforehand and ask them to learn detailed definitions for each term. As part of your exam, list the definitions that you have constructed yourself (or copied from your text's glossary) for some of the terms that were distributed. Ask your students to write the name of the correct term beside each definition without using their lists as a memory aid. Two points can be assigned for a correct spelling, one point for an incorrect but recognizable spelling. Reverse IDs can be graded much more quickly than regular IDs and, because students' study time beforehand is guided, they help promote learning of the basic vocabulary of a discipline, a common objective in most large introductory courses.

Essays. It is essential that the length of students' answers be limited if essays are to be used in large sections. Good ways to do this are to focus the questions somewhat more than you would in a smaller class, to encourage students to be terse, and to give them a limited amount of space in which to answer. Rarely are students' rambling essays so wonderful that they will be harmed by asking them to confine their prose, especially if the question can be managed in that space. Essay questions can be used in a large section but are best modified to make them shorter and quicker to grade.

Common Out-of-Class Methods

Outside writing assignments meet many desirable educational objectives. It would be unfortunate to omit them from consideration in a large class because of the grading time they would require. As is true of in-class essay exams, writing assignments can still be used in large classes if instructors modify the assignment somewhat.

Consider the following ways to structure writing assignments:
- Make term papers optional (rarely will more than one-third of a large section choose to write a paper, even if you average it into the final grade on a par with each exam)
- Ask for shorter forms of written work from all students (for example, reaction papers, reading journals, position papers, laboratory, or observational reports have worked well for others)
- Assign group projects that will produce a smaller number of written products to grade.

When considering out-of-class assignments, ask yourself if it is essential that everything that we ask students to do be graded. If anything, a LO is more likely to be encouraged if students can be motivated to seek some outside educational experience for the internal satisfaction it will give, not just to receive credit toward their final grade. (See Lowman, 1984, for a more detailed discussion of this topic.) Recommending that students attend lectures or concerts or visit sites of relevance to your course and giving them an opportunity to tell you (orally or in writing) about their experience may promote a desirable attitude toward their learning that far outweighs the fact an opportunity was missed to give them a grade.

Conclusion

A large class is unlikely to be satisfying to students or to instructors unless accommodations are made for the size of the room, the larger numbers of students to know and control, and the inevitable diffusion of individual responsibility for the success of the learning experience. Sheer economy of scale will require modifications in methods of evaluating and giving feedback to students regardless of an instructors' objectives or ideals. Unless instructors actively seek to meet this challenge, evaluation procedures can result that promote a grading orientation and a gamesmanship attitude toward exams. Structuring evaluation to be only one segment of a feedback loop in which students know what is expected beforehand, how well they succeeded afterward, and what they can do to improve in the future is far more likely to be satisfying than letting practical pressures dictate one-way evaluation methods.

References

Baker, P. J., and Behrens, P. J. "Alternatives to Mass Instruction in Sociology." *The American Sociologist*, 1971, *6*, 311–317.

Bloom, B. S. (ed.). *Taxonomy of Educational Objectives: Cognitive Domain*. New York: Longmans, Green, 1956.

Eisen, J. "A New Instrument for Assessing Students' Orientations Toward Grades and Learning." *Psychological Reports*, 1981, *48*, 919–924.

Furhman, B. S., and Grasha, A. F. *A Practical Handbook for College Teachers*. Boston: Little, Brown, 1983.

Haladyna, T. M., and Downing, S. M. "An Analysis of Knowledge about Multiple-Choice Test Item Writing." Paper presented at the 97th meeting of the American Psychological Association, Toronto, 1984.

Lowman, J. *Mastering the Techniques of Teaching*. San Francisco: Jossey-Bass, 1984.

Lunneborg, P. *College Grades: What Do Professors Intend to Communicate?* Seattle: Assessment Center, University of Washington, 1977.

McGee, R. "Practical Problems of Mass Instruction: A Personal Memorandum." In R. McGee (ed.), *Teaching the Mass Class*. Washington, D.C.: American Sociological Association, 1986.

McKeachie, W. *Teaching Tips*. Lexington, Mass.: Heath, 1978.

Milton, O., Pollio, H. R., and Eisen, J. A. *Making Sense of College Grades: Why the Grading System Does Not Work and What Can Be Done About It*. San Francisco: Jossey-Bass, 1986.

Semb, G., and Spencer, R. "Beyond the Level of Recall: An Analysis of Higher Order Educational Tasks." In L. Fraley and E. Vargas (eds.), *Proceedings of the Third National Conference on Behavior and Technology in Higher Education*. Atlanta: Georgia State University, 1976.

Shaw, M. E., and Costanzo, P. R. *Theories of Social Psychology*. New York: McGraw-Hill, 1982.

Joseph Lowman is professor in the department of psychology at the University of North Carolina, Chapel Hill. He is author of Mastering the Techniques of Teaching *(Jossey-Bass, 1984).*

There are good reasons for expecting informative feedback to
have beneficial effects on teaching performance in large classes.

Acquiring Student Feedback
That Improves Instruction

Harry G. Murray

Student evaluation of teaching has taken on increased importance in
North American colleges and universities over the past twenty years. Seldin (1984) reported that the percentage of liberal arts colleges using student ratings as an index of faculty teaching performance had increased
from 29 percent in 1973 to 53 percent in 1978 and to 67 percent in 1983.
Knapper (1986) found that 95 percent of psychology departments in Canadian universities used student instructional ratings on a regular basis.

      Generally, student evaluation of teaching takes the form of a struc-
tured, multiple-choice questionnaire assessing characteristics such as clarity of explanation, organization of materials, fairness of exams, and
encouragement of student participation. In most institutions, the results
of student evaluation are used for one or both of two major purposes: as
diagnostic feedback intended to bring about improvement in faculty teaching performance—usually referred to as *formative evaluation;* and as input
to administrative decisions on faculty retention, tenure, promotion, and
merit pay—generally known as *summative evaluation.* Although not necessarily incompatible, these are very different purposes, and they should
be kept separate, both conceptually and procedurally. One obvious difference between summative and formative evaluation is that the former is
far more threatening and controversial than the latter. While virtually all

M. G. Weimer (ed.). *Teaching Large Classes Well.*
New Directions for Teaching and Learning, no. 32. San Francisco: Jossey-Bass, Winter 1987.

faculty members are in favor of student evaluation of teaching for the sole purpose of improving performance, the use of student ratings in decisions on job security and career progress continues to be a matter of heated debate. In a survey of faculty members at the University of Western Ontario, Murray and others (1982) found that providing diagnostic feedback was rated as a highly important goal of teaching evaluation by 78 percent of respondents, whereas providing information for personnel decisions was rated as highly important by only 42 percent of respondents. A second difference between summative and formative evaluation is that different types of student rating forms are appropriate for these two purposes. The most useful instrument for administrative personnel decisions is a standardized rating form focusing on global, widely applicable characteristics that are under the instructor's direct control. But a global rating form of this type is of limited value for self-improvement purposes, because it says nothing about idiosyncratic factors in teaching, fails to specify the reasons for low ratings, and provides no specific suggestions for improvement. Faculty dissatisfaction and frustration can arise when, as is commonly the case, a global evaluation form designed for summative use is forced to do double duty in a formative role.

This chapter is concerned solely with formative evaluation of teaching. Specifically, the goal is to examine ways of obtaining diagnostic feedback that will lead to improved teaching in large, lecture-type classes. Informative feedback, or knowledge of results, has been found to improve human performance in many different contexts (Annett, 1969). There are good reasons for expecting informative feedback to have similar beneficial effects on teaching performance in large classes.

Impact of Student Feedback

Given that faculty members are generally in favor of formative evaluation of teaching, and given that students are available to perform this service, the question arises as to whether students represent the best source of diagnostic feedback. Certainly there are alternative sources of feedback, including self-evaluation, classroom observation by colleagues or supervisors, videotaping or audiotaping, and expert consultation. While each of these methods has its unique merits and each can be used advantageously in combination with input from students, there are strong arguments for relying on student feedback as the primary impetus for instructional improvement. For one thing, research indicates that student ratings can provide reliable and valid information on certain aspects of classroom teaching. Although results vary somewhat from study to study, the weight of evidence indicates that student ratings of a given instructor show high interrater (among raters) and retest reliability, are affected to only a minor extent by extraneous factors such as class size, are consistent with comparable ratings made by alumni and trained classroom observers, and are positively correlated with more objective measures of teaching effectiveness, such as student performance on standardized examinations (Marsh, 1984; Murray, 1980). It is interesting to note that Centra (1975) found that student ratings showed higher levels of interrater agreement than colleague ratings of the same instructors. Second, because students observe teaching on a day-to-day basis throughout the academic term, and because students represent a "normal" or "natural" aspect of the classroom environment, it can be argued that student assessment of teaching is both less obtrusive and less subject to sampling error than assessment based on videotaping or classroom visitation. Third, student feedback is superior in terms of cost effectiveness, in that one can obtain a large amount of feedback data at a small cost in time, effort, and money. A final advantage of student feedback, which applies particularly in large classes, is that the mere act of soliciting input from students serves to open communication lines between teacher and students and thus to counteract the atmosphere of impersonality and alienation that exists in many college classrooms.

Potential advantages notwithstanding, it would be reassuring to know that feedback from students does in fact produce improvement in quality of teaching. Empirical evidence supporting this assertion is provided by field research in which student feedback is manipulated experimentally. A typical experiment of this type involves random assignment of teachers to an experimental group that receives mid-term student feedback and to a control group that receives no feedback. The two groups are then compared on global end-of-term student ratings to assess whether feedback has any beneficial effect. In a variation on this basic design, McKeachie and others (1980) compared groups of teachers who, at mid-semester, received either no student feedback; a standard computer printout of student item ratings plus norms; or a computer printout supplemented by individual consultation with an expert teacher who interpreted the printout, provided motivational support, and offered specific suggestions for improvement. The three groups differed significantly in end-of-semester student ratings, with the feedback-plus-consultation group showing the highest ratings, the feedback-only group performing at an intermediate level, and the no-feedback group receiving the lowest ratings. In other words, student feedback alone led to modest improvement in teaching, whereas student feedback supplemented by expert consultation produced a much larger gain in quality of teaching. Overall and Marsh (1979) found that student feedback plus expert consultation had beneficial effects on criterion measures other than end-of-term ratings—for example, student examination performance and plans to take further courses. Stevens and Aleamoni (1985) reported that the impact of student feedback plus follow-up consultation can persist for as long as

ten years. Cohen (1980) conducted a meta-analysis of twenty-two published studies of student feedback effectiveness. He found that instructors
receiving mid-term feedback scored higher than control instructors on
end-of-term ratings in twenty of twenty-two studies, with this difference
reaching statistical significance in ten of twenty-two studies. Across all
studies, the mean gain in end-of-term ratings due to student feedback
alone was approximately .10 points on a 5-point scale, or 8 percentile
points, whereas the mean gain due to student feedback supplemented by
expert consultation was approximately .33 rating scale points, or 24 percentile points. Thus an instructor starting at the fiftieth percentile in
end-of-term student ratings would be expected to improve to the fifty-
eighth percentile as a result of student feedback alone, and to improve to
the seventy-fourth percentile as a result of student feedback plus expert
consultation. Cohen's conclusions were generally supported by Menges
and Brinko's (1986) more recent meta-analysis of student feedback studies.
There is clear evidence, then, that student feedback can produce significant improvement in quality of teaching, particularly if feedback is
supplemented by expert consultation.

Further evidence that student feedback leads to improvement of
teaching comes from surveys of faculty attitudes on instructional evaluation. In the largest survey of this type to date, Outcalt (1980) found that
67 percent of 4,468 faculty respondents at the University of California
believed student ratings had helped them improve their teaching, whereas
78 percent said they had made specific changes in their teaching as a
result of student ratings. Similarly, Gross and Small (1979) found that
84 percent of faculty at George Mason University thought that student
instructional ratings had led to instructional improvement. Of eight
faculty surveys known to the author, all but one have supported the
formative value of student feedback.

Behavioral Feedback

Given that student feedback can improve teaching, the next question is what type of feedback is most beneficial for this purpose. For
example, should feedback be instructor-oriented or course-oriented,
should it be standardized or idiosyncratic, and should it be in the form
of prose comments or multiple-choice ratings? These questions have
received scant attention in the research literature. None of the field experiments reviewed by Cohen (1980) appear to have directly compared the
effectiveness of different types of student feedback.

Ory and Braskamp (1981) and Murray and others (1982)
approached this issue by surveying faculty perceptions of the relative usefulness of alternative feedback formats. Ory and Braskamp found that
open-ended prose comments from students were viewed as less compre-

hensive and more difficult to interpret than structured ratings of global characteristics, but nonetheless as more believable and more useful for self-improvement purposes than global ratings. Murray and others reported that student ratings of specific teaching behaviors were viewed by faculty as most useful for diagnostic purposes (78 percent endorsement), whereas prose comments were next most useful (65 percent endorsement), and global ratings were least useful (54 percent endorsement).

Faculty preference for specific behavioral feedback in the Murray and others (1982) study provides a hint as to why student feedback alone produced relatively small gains in perceived teaching effectiveness in the field experiments reviewed by Cohen (1980). In most of these experiments, mid-term feedback consisted of mean student ratings of global instructor characteristics such as "clarity," "rapport," and "overall effectiveness." Low ratings on items of this sort inform the teacher that something is wrong, but provide no indication of the specific classroom behaviors that gave rise to the problem or the specific changes that will bring about improvement. On the other hand, low ratings on specific behavioral items such as "maintains eye contact with students," "indicates the transition from one topic to the next," and "uses frequent examples," provide a clear signal as to what is wrong and what remedial action is needed. According to this analysis, the reason student feedback plus expert consultation produced large instructional gains is that the expert consultant was able to interpret global student ratings in specific behavioral terms and to recommend specific behavioral change strategies. One would expect, then, that a student feedback form that focuses on specific classroom teaching behaviors would minimize the need for external consultation and would be more effective in improving teaching than a traditional global feedback form.

One prerequisite for the success of a student feedback form focusing on specific instructional behaviors is that the behaviors in question can be reliably judged by students. A second prerequisite is that the instructional behaviors are significantly related to outcome measures of teaching effectiveness, such as student satisfaction and student achievement. Research conducted by the author and by other investigators suggests that both of these presuppositions are viable. Murray (1983a) reported interrater reliability coefficients ranging from .24 to .97 (median = .76) for student estimates of the frequency of occurrence of 60 specific classroom behaviors in a sample of social science lecturers. In other words, students showed moderate to high levels of interobserver agreement in rating specific instructional behaviors.

Moreover, Murray found that 26 of 60 classroom behaviors, representing seven different behavioral factors or underlying dimensions, correlated significantly with student ratings of overall instructor effectiveness. Correlations with overall effectiveness were highest for behaviors related to "enthusiasm" and "clarity" factors. The enthusiasm factor included speaking expressively, using movement and gesture, and maintaining eye contact with students, which were hypothesized to elicit and maintain student attention to the lecturer's presentation. The clarity factor included giving multiple examples, using graphs and diagrams, and stressing important points, which were assumed to assist student comprehension of concepts. Consistent with these results, Tom and Cushman (1975) reported significant correlations between student reports of twenty-eight different teaching behaviors, including vocal expressiveness, signaling the transition to new topics, stating lecture objectives, and student self-ratings of amount learned in agriculture courses. Murray (1983b) showed that classroom teaching behaviors are related to measures of teaching effectiveness other than end-of-term students ratings—for example, student achievement and motivation for further study. Finally, Erdle and Murray (1986) demonstrated that correlations between teaching behaviors and rated effectiveness are consistent across different academic disciplines.

Two previous studies have attempted, each with limited success, to demonstrate improvement in teaching as a result of student feedback on specific classroom behaviors. Froman and Owen (1980) found no significant differences in end-of-semester student ratings among randomly assigned groups of teachers who, at mid-semester, received either no student feedback, feedback on ten global characteristics such as "stimulates interest," feedback on sixty-eight specific instructional behaviors such as "presents material at too fast a pace," or feedback on both global characteristics and specific behaviors. There are several possible reasons for the nonsignificant impact of behavioral feedback in the Froman and Owen study. For one thing, given that classroom teaching behaviors are acquired over a period of many years, it may be unreasonable to expect significant change in these behaviors within a time frame of only six to eight weeks. Second, the feedback provided on specific instructional behaviors in the Froman and Owen study was very limited in terms of implications for improvement. Only those classroom behaviors checked by at least 25 percent of students as "particularly notable" were reported to the instructor as feedback. For example, an instructor might be informed that 32 percent of students viewed "stresses important points" as a notable characteristic of his or her classroom teaching. This type of feedback is of limited value for formative purposes, as it fails to specify whether the behavior in question is in need of improvement, and if so, whether the behavior needs to be increased or decreased in frequency. Also, no information is provided on teaching behaviors checked by less than 25 percent of students.

In a second study of the impact of mid-term behavioral feedback, McLean (1979) obtained weekly student ratings of overall teaching effectiveness for volunteer experimental and control teachers during six-week periods preceding and following the receipt of behavioral feedback by experimental teachers. Feedback consisted of mean student frequency-of-occurrence estimates (1 = never, 3 = sometimes, 5 = always) for one hundred specific classroom behaviors. Frequency estimates were accompanied by percentile norms that allowed instructors to compare themselves to others teaching similar courses, and information on the magnitude and direction of correlations between teaching behaviors and overall effectiveness ratings in previous research. Although experimental teachers expressed generally favorable attitudes toward behavioral feedback and believed that their teaching had improved as a result of feedback, there was no significant difference between experimental and control teachers in pretest-to-posttest gains in rated teaching effectiveness. However, follow-up analysis showed that experimental teachers whose prefeedback ratings ranked in the bottom third of the sample showed significant improvement following feedback, whereas middle- and high-ranked teachers showed no significant improvement. McLean suggested that poorer teachers tend to be unaware of their own classroom behaviors and thus are more in need of specific behavioral feedback than their higher-rated colleagues. Statistical regression was not seen as a viable interpretation of the improved performance of low-rated teachers because performance gains were restricted to observation periods following the introduction of feedback and were not apparent in repeated prefeedback observations.

In summary, the McLean study yielded slightly more positive results than the Froman and Owen study, but the case for behavioral feedback was still rather weak. Moreover, the same methodological limitations cited above in relation to the Froman and Owen study seem to apply with equal force to the McLean study. First, McLean used a postfeedback period of only six weeks, which is probably too short for detecting changes in well-established teaching behaviors. Second, although behavioral feedback was thorough and well-structured in the McLean study, it is possible that the quantitative information provided, which included elaborate statistical norms, was too complex and difficult to interpret to be useful for improvement of teaching.

Teacher Behaviors Inventory

Despite the pessimistic results of research to date, behavioral feedback continues to have strong potential for improving college and university teaching, and it would be premature to abandon research and development in this area. As noted previously, diagnostic feedback from students is particularly important in large, lecture-type courses where direct teacher-student interaction tends to be infrequent. Figure 1 is an instrument developed by the author to fill the need for useful behavioral feedback in large lecture courses. The Teacher Behaviors Inventory (TBI):

Figure 1. Teacher Behaviors Inventory: Diagnostic Version

Instructions to Student

In this inventory you are asked to assess your instructor's specific classroom behaviors. Your instructor has requested this information for purposes of instructional analysis and improvement. A statistical summary of results will be provided to your instructor. No one else will have access to these data without your instructor's consent. Please try to be both thoughtful and candid in your responses so as to maximize the value of feedback.

Each section of the inventory begins with a definition of the category of teaching to be assessed in that section. For each specific teaching behavior, please indicate your judgment as to whether your instructor should increase, decrease, or make no change in the frequency with which he/she exhibits the behavior in question. Please use the following rating scale in making your judgments:

–2—large decrease in frequency needed
–1—small decrease in frequency needed
 0—no change in frequency needed
+1—small increase in frequency needed
+2—large increase in frequency needed

Mark your ratings on the answer sheet provided, using a soft lead pencil only. Your judgments should reflect that type of teaching you think is best for this particular course and your particular learning style. Try to assess each behavior independently rather than letting your overall impression of the instructor determine each individual rating.

Clarity: methods used to explain or clarify concepts and principles

 1. gives several examples of each concept
 2. uses concrete everyday examples to explain concepts and principles
 3. fails to define new or unfamiliar terms
 4. repeats difficult ideas several times
 5. stresses most important points by pausing, speaking slowly, raising voice, and so on
 6. uses graphs or diagrams to facilitate explanation
 7. points out practical applications of concepts
 8. answers students' questions thoroughly
 9. suggests ways of memorizing complicated ideas
10. writes key terms on blackboard or overhead screen
11. explains subject matter in familiar colloquial language

Enthusiasm: use of nonverbal behavior to solicit student attention and interest

12. speaks in a dramatic or expressive way
13. moves about while lecturing
14. gestures with hands or arms
15. exhibits facial gestures or expressions
16. avoids eye contact with students
17. walks up aisles beside students

18. gestures with head or body
19. tells jokes or humorous anecdotes
20. reads lecture verbatim from prepared notes or text
21. smiles or laughs while teaching
22. shows distracting mannerisms

Interaction: techniques used to foster student participation in class

23. encourages students to ask questions or make comments during lectures
24. criticizes students when they make errors
25. praises students for good ideas
26. asks questions of individual students
27. asks questions of class as a whole
28. incorporates students' ideas into lecture
29. presents challenging, thought-provoking ideas
30. uses a variety of media and activities in class
31. asks rhetorical questions

Organization: ways of organizing or structuring subject matter of course

32. uses headings and subheadings to organize lectures
33. puts outline of lecture on blackboard or overhead screen
34. clearly indicates transition from one topic to the next
35. gives preliminary overview of lecture at beginning of class
36. explains how each topic fits into the course as a whole
37. reviews topics covered in previous lecture at beginning of each class
38. periodically summarizes points previously made

Pacing: rate of presentation of information, efficient use of class time

39. dwells excessively on obvious points
40. digresses from major theme of lecture
41. covers very little material in class sessions
42. asks if students understand before proceeding to next topic
43. sticks to the point in answering students' questions

Disclosure: explicitness concerning course requirements and grading criteria

44. advises students as to how to prepare for tests or exams
45. provides sample exam questions
46. tells students exactly what is expected of them on tests, essays, or assignments
47. states objectives of each lecture
48. reminds students of test dates or assignment deadlines
49. states objectives of course as a whole

Speech: characteristics of voice relevant to classroom teaching

50. stutters, mumbles, or slurs words
51. speaks at appropriate volume
52. speaks clearly
53. speaks at appropriate pace
54. says "um" or "ah"
55. voice lacks proper modulation (speaks in monotone)

Figure 1. *(continued)*

Rapport: quality of interpersonal relations between teacher and students

56. addresses individual students by name
57. announces availability for consultation outside of class
58. offers to help students with problems
59. shows tolerance of other points of view
60. talks with students before or after class

Source: This inventory was developed by Professor H. G. Murray, Department of Psychology, University of Western Ontario. It is not copyrighted and may be reproduced for any valid research or instructional development purpose.

Diagnostic Version is based on previous research by the author on classroom teaching behaviors (Murray, 1983a, 1983b, 1985) and incorporates design improvements suggested by the failure of prior behavioral feedback studies (Froman and Owen, 1980; McLean, 1979).

The diagnostic version of the TBI consists of sixty items, each referring to a specific classroom teaching behavior that has been found in at least one previous study to show an interrater reliability coefficient of at least .60 and a significant correlation with student evaluation of overall teaching effectiveness. Students rate each of the sixty classroom teaching behaviors on a five-point scale to indicate whether, for purposes of instructional improvement, the behavior in question needs to be increased in frequency of occurrence (positive rating), decreased in frequency (negative rating), or unchanged in frequency (zero rating). It is anticipated that a rating scale of this type will provide behavioral feedback that is more simple, direct, easy to interpret, and obvious in its implications for improvement than the behavioral feedback used in the Froman and Owen (1980) and McLean (1979) studies. With results averaged across students, the instructor can obtain specific suggestions for improvement simply by identifying TBI items whose mean ratings deviate noticeably from zero.

Although no formal research has been done on the diagnostic Teacher Behaviors Inventory to date, it is recommended for trial use by instructors seeking behavioral feedback for improvement of teaching. Instructors are advised to pay heed to the following guidelines in using the diagnostic TBI for instructional improvement:

1. The diagnostic TBI is most appropriate for courses using a lecture or lecture-discussion style of teaching. Instructors wishing to use the TBI for non-lecture courses may delete or substitute items as they see fit, but no advance assurance can be provided in such cases regarding statistical reliability of results.

2. The TBI is intended to be used for instructional improvement on a continuous, long-term basis. Instructors are advised to obtain feedback regularly over a period of several academic terms, rather than

on a one-shot basis, and to monitor present versus prior results in a systematic way.

3. The TBI was developed for use by individual instructors seeking feedback on their own teaching. The evaluation results should be the sole property of the instructor in question, unless he or she agrees to the contrary.

4. Ideally, the instrument should be completed by all students in the class. If this is not feasible, data should be obtained from a random sample of at least fifteen students.

5. Analysis of results should consist of, at minimum, computation of the mean (average) and standard deviation of ratings for each item. This can be done by a computer software package such as SPSS, or by a simple desk calculator.

6. In interpreting item means and standard deviations, the most useful strategy would be to look for items with mean ratings of higher than +0.50 or lower than −0.50, for example, and relatively small standard deviations. These are items on which there is general agreement among students that either an increase or decrease in behavioral frequency is needed.

References

Annett, J. *Feedback and Human Behavior*. Harmondsworth, England: Penguin, 1969.

Centra, J. A. "Colleagues as Raters of Classroom Instruction." *Journal of Higher Education*, 1975, *46*, 327–337.

Cohen, P. A. "Effectiveness of Student-Rating Feedback for Improving College Instruction: A Meta-Analysis of Findings." *Research in Higher Education*, 1980, *13*, 321–341.

Erdle, S., and Murray, H. G. "Interfaculty Differences in Classroom Teaching Behaviors and Their Relationship to Student Instructional Ratings." *Research in Higher Education*, 1986, *24*, 115–127.

Froman, R. D., and Owen, S. V. *Influence of Different Types of Student Ratings Feedback upon Later Instructional Behavior*. Paper presented at annual meeting of the American Educational Research Association, Boston, April 1980.

Gross, R. B., and Small, A. C. "A Survey of Faculty Opinions About Student Evaluations of Instructors." *Teaching of Psychology*, 1979, *6*, 216–219.

Knapper, C. K. "A Survey of Instructional Practices in Canadian Psychology Departments." *Canadian Psychology*, 1986, *27* (1), 51–62.

Marsh, H. W. "Students' Evaluations of University Teaching: Dimensionality, Reliability, Validity, Potential Biases, and Utility." *Journal of Educational Psychology*, 1984, *76*, 707–754.

McKeachie, W. J., Lin, Y. G., Daugherty, M., Moffett, M. M., Neigler, C., Nork, J., Walz, M., and Baldwin, R. "Using Student Ratings and Consultation to Improve Instruction." *British Journal of Educational Psychology*, 1980, *50*, 168–174.

McLean, D. F. *The Effect of Midsemester Feedback upon Weekly Evaluations of University Instructors*. Unpublished master's thesis, University of Western Ontario, London, Canada, 1979.

Menges, R. J., and Brinko, K. T. *Effects of Student Evaluation Feedback: A Meta-Analysis of Higher Education Research*. Paper presented at the meeting of the American Educational Research Association, San Francisco, 1986.

Murray, H. G. *Evaluating University Teaching: A Review of Research*. Toronto: Ontario Confederation of University Faculty Associations, 1980.

Murray, H. G. "Low-Inference Classroom Teaching Behaviors and Student Ratings of College Teaching Effectiveness." *Journal of Educational Psychology,* 1983a, *75,* 138–149.

Murray, H. G. *Low-Inference Classroom Teaching Behaviors in Relation to Six Measures of College Teaching Effectiveness*. Paper presented at the Conference on the Evaluation and Improvement of University Teaching, Montebello, Quebec, Canada, November 1983b.

Murray, H. G. "Classroom Teaching Behaviors Related to College Teaching Effectiveness." In J. G. Donald and A. M. Sullivan (eds.), *Using Research to Improve Teaching*. New Directions for Teaching and Learning, no. 23. San Francisco: Jossey-Bass, 1985.

Murray, H. G., Newby, W. G., Bowden, B., Crealock, C., Gaily, T. D., Oswin, J., and Smith, P. "Evaluation of Teaching at the University of Western Ontario, "Report to Provost's Advisory, Committee on Teaching and Learning, University of Western Ontario, July 1982.

Ory, J. C., and Braskamp, L. A. "Faculty Perceptions of the Quality and Usefulness of Three Types of Evaluative Information." *Research in Higher Education,* 1981, *15,* 271–282.

Outcalt, D. L. (ed.). *Report of the Task Force on Teaching Evaluation*. Berkeley: The University of California, 1980.

Overall, J. U., and Marsh, H. W. "Midterm Feedback from Students: Its Relationship to Instructional Improvement and Students' Cognitive and Affective Outcomes." *Journal of Educational Psychology,* 1979, *71,* 856–865.

Seldin, P. *Changing Practices in Faculty Evaluation: A Critical Assessment and Recommendations for Improvement*. San Francisco: Jossey-Bass, 1984.

Stevens, J. J., and Aleamoni, L. M. "The Use of Evaluative Feedback for Instructional Improvement: A Longitudinal Perspective." *Instructional Science,* 1985, *13,* 285–304.

Tom, F.K.T., and Cushman, H. R. "The Cornell Diagnostic Observation and Reporting System for Student Description of College Teaching." *Search,* 1975, *5* (8), 1–27.

Harry G. Murray is a member of the faculty of social science in the department of psychology at the University of Western Ontario.

This bibliography consists of materials written specifically for those teaching large classes and contains material offering sound, practical advice.

A Bibliography of Ideas for Practitioners

Maryellen Gleason Weimer, Mary-Margaret Kerns

A fitting way to conclude this volume is by offering an annotated bibliography of additional sources for faculty who teach large classes. Several criteria influenced decisions about the kind of resources faculty would find useful. This is not a general bibliography on teaching and learning or on research literature. Collections of material on these topics are readily accessible elsewhere, including other volumes in this series. To date, the primary topic related to large classes that has been subjected to empirical investigation has been the impact of class size on student learning and satisfaction. The findings are interesting but inconclusive and, for the time being, not likely to affect current practices. At least for the foreseeable future, especially at our large public institutions, students will receive part of their education in courses enrolling many students.

Therefore, what follows is a bibliography of material written specifically about large classes, emphasizing sound, practical advice. Discovering material that met this criterion was not difficult. Much of what has been written about teaching large classes has been written for practitioners by practitioners. What is proposed in the bibliography is not supported by references to related research. However, the strategies, techniques, advice, and ideas are credible by virtue of the authors' having proven that they work in large classes.

M. G. Weimer (ed.). *Teaching Large Classes Well.*
New Directions for Teaching and Learning, no. 32. San Francisco: Jossey-Bass, Winter 1987.

Much of the literature on teaching large classes has been published in discipline-specific, pedagogical journals. These tend not be read outside the discipline, because instructors tend to view the challenges of their own field as being unique. In reality, an American history teacher in a class of 150 has much in common with a physics teacher in a class of 200. Faculty teaching large classes should look for advice and ideas across disciplinary boundaries. Many of the instructional challenges created by big classes transcend individual academic areas. Granted, the approach of the physicist will have to be modified by the historian but frequently not as much as might be suspected. The bibliography contains a number of sources that provide potentially transferable and transformable techniques and strategies.

Material in the bibliography is organized around issues that frequently concern instructors teaching large courses. A brief and sometimes partisan annotation is included for each reference.

Being Able to Teach Without Always Having to Lecture

Bergquist, W. H., and Phillips, S. R. *A Handbook for Faculty Development.* Vol. I. Washington, D.C. The Council for the Advancement of Small Colleges, 1975.

See pages 118–121 for a table listing and describing thirteen classroom structures that encourage student participation.

Bowman, J. S. "The Lecture-Discussion Format Revisited." *Improving College and University Teaching,* 1979, 27 (1), 25–27.

With this revisit, the author concludes that the lecture-discussion method as used in mass instructional settings has much to offer. It can be used successfully; the chapter tells you how.

Brooks, D. W. "Alternatives to Traditional Lecturing." *Journal of Chemical Education,* 1984, *61* (10), 858–859.

A variety of alternatives are proposed. The author has used them successfully in courses enrolling more than two hundred students.

Michaelsen, L. K. "Team Learning in Large Classes." In C. Bouton and R. Y. Garth (eds.), *Learning in Groups.* New Directions for Teaching and Learning, no. 14. San Francisco: Jossey-Bass, 1983.

"Team learning is an instructional format . . . [that makes] extensive use in the classroom of permanent, heterogeneous, six- or seven-member student learning groups" (p. 13). The articles include a variety of details on the groups including how to form them, make them cohesive, use them in classroom activities, and grade them.

Pultorak, R. W. "The Colloqution Module: Rx for Somnifacient Lectures." *Journal of College Science Teaching,* 1985, *14* (5), 421–423.

The author suggests ways of using groups that involve students in activities related to reading assignments. The idea offers a break from lecturing and makes it more likely that students will do the reading (a decidedly added bonus).

Smith, W. M. "The Use of PSI in Large-Course Instruction." In G. L. Wolford and W. M. Smith (eds), *Large-Course Instruction.* Hanover, N.H. Office of Instructional Services and Educational Research and Department of Psychology, Darthmouth College, 1975.

The article is really not a "how to" for potential PSI users but provides a theoretical and practical background for PSI. If you don't know that PSI stands for Personalized System of Instruction, this article orients you to the approach.

Stanton, H. E. "Small Group Teaching in the Lecture Situation." *Improving College and University Teaching,* 1978, *26* (1), 69–70.

A specific proposal for incorporating group work within a lecture presentation is offered by this author. He includes concrete advice for lecturers inexperienced in using in-class group activities.

Weaver, R. L., II. "The Small Group in Large Classes." *The Educational Forum,* 1983, *48* (1), 65–73.

The author proposes and describes five uses for small-group discussion in large classes: (1) to illustrate material students are assigned to read, (2) to develop new ideas or models, (3) to develop or extend lecture material, (4) to solve problems, and (5) to examine students.

Large Audiences Are Unnerving

Bain, R. K. "On Making It Play in Peoria." In R. McGee (ed.), *Teaching the Mass Class.* Washington, D.C.: American Sociological Association, 1986.

"Teaching a large class sometimes reminds me of steering an ocean liner with a canoe paddle; a change of course is small and delayed." But the author does offer some effective and innovative "paddles"—especially pertaining to both desirable and undesirable student involvement in the lecture.

Gleason, M. "Better Communication in Large Courses." *College Teaching,* 1986, *34* (1), 20–24.

This paper looks at five environmental conditions that impede effective communication in large classes. It proposes a variety of techniques instructors can use to overcome the barriers.

Kain, E. "The Mass Class as Theatre—Suggestions for Improving the Chances of a Hit Production." In R. McGee (ed.), *Teaching the Mass Class.* Washington, D.C.: American Sociological Association, 1986.

Sometimes faculty object to the theatre metaphor and the notion that teaching has anything in common with show business. In this case don't be bothered by the title. The author proposes useful and logically backed suggestions, which are just what the less entertaining and meeker/milder faculty need.

Getting Students to Think

Monk, G. S. "Student Engagement and Teacher Power in Large Classes." In C. Bouton and R. Y. Garth (eds.), *Learning in Groups.* New Directions for Teaching and Learning, no. 14. San Francisco: Jossey-Bass, 1983.

A math instructor recounts how he restructured his math course with the aim of forcing students to work through basic courses' procedures and concepts. Also offers good advice on using TAs.

Moss, G. D., and McMillen, D. "A Strategy for Developing Problem-Solving Skills in Large Undergraduate Classes." *Studies in Higher Education,* 1980, 5 (2), 161–171.

The strategy utilizes a problem involving foreign policy formulation. That limits its applicability to some content areas but the structure could be modified. The strategy develops problem-solving skills.

Providing Quality Learning Experiences in Introductory Courses

Brock, S. C. "Practitioners' Views on Teaching the Large Introductory College Course." Manhattan, Kansas: Center for Faculty Evaluation and Development, 1976.

Fifteen instructors were asked to identify "the special pedagogical problems faced by teachers of the large introductory course." They were also asked to offer solutions and general recommendations. Their responses are contained in this nine-page document.

Dunham, R. E., and Gleason, M. "Challenges of the Introductory Course." In K. I. Spear (ed.), *Rejuvenating Introductory Courses.* New Directions for Teaching and Learning, no. 20. San Francisco: Jossey-Bass, 1984.

Beginning with a review of goals of introductory courses, the authors then look at how those purposes can be accomplished given the constraints imposed by such factors as large enrollments.

The Impersonal Climate of the Large Class

Kogut, L. S. "Quality Circles: A Japanese Management Technique for the Classroom." *Improving College and University Teaching*, 1984, *32* (3), 123-127.

This instructor teaches large sections of introductory chemistry. He uses quality circles as a means of keeping his finger on the pulse of a large section.

Pardy, R. L., and Mortensen, L. "The Biology Hot Line: Use of a Telephone Answering Device in Large Classes." *Improving College and University Teaching*, 1984, *32* (4), 188-190.

The author recounts experiences using an answering machine in a 300-student human physiology course. Students were encouraged to ask questions or comment on course-related matters such as lecture material, laboratory exercises, reading assignments, and test grades.

Making the Most of Teaching Assistants

Hazeltine, B. "Undergraduate TAs in Big Courses—Everybody Wins." *Engineering Education*, 1981, *71* (5), 363-365.

This author explains that undergraduate TAs have been used successfully in an electronics circuit course and a management course. He claims, "A student's confidence is boosted by seeing that a person only slightly more experienced has mastered the material."

Parrot, A. "Structuring a Large Human Sexuality Class to Provide Students with the Personal Contact of a Small Class." In R. McGee (ed.), *Teaching the Mass Class*. Washington, D.C.: American Sociological Association, 1986.

This chapter provides an organizational structure and delineates responsibilities for instructors and TAs. While not applicable in all academic fields, instructors in many areas besides human sexuality, such as human development, health, and recreation would benefit from reviewing this detailed description of course structure.

Sundgren, A. S. "Working the Crowd: Organizing and Controlling the Mass Class." In R. McGee (ed.), *Teaching the Mass Class*. Washington, D.C.: American Sociological Association, 1986.

This chapter is included because it contains a first-rate section on organizing TAs.

Providing Good Feedback with Limited Time
to Devote to Grading

Kabel, R. L. "Ideas for Managing Large Classes," *Engineering Education*, 1983, *74* (2), 80-83.

The author shares how he handles assignments and grading in a 120-student kinetics and industrial chemistry course. His system includes a variety of innovative strategies applicable to other problem-solving courses.

Wolford, G. L. "Assessment of Student Performance." In G. L. Wolford and W. M. Smith (eds.), *Large Course Instruction.* Hanover, N.H.: Office of Instructional Services and Educational Research, Department of Psychology, Dartmouth College, 1975.
   The author treats the reliability and validity of grading different types of tests and discusses some of the crucial issues related to use of multiple graders.

Doing the Best Possible Job

Brass, D., and Gioia, D. "Never Wear Your Pink Shirt in the Forum: Student Evaluations of Teaching the Large Course." *Organizational Behavior Teaching Journal,* 1985, *91,* 100–103.
   This chapter contains a report of how two instructors who team teach a 400-student course used evaluations to improve their instruction.

King, J. H., and Lindsay, E. J. "Evaluation of Teaching Effectiveness in Large Courses." In G. L. Wolford, and W. M. Smith (eds.), *Large Course Instruction.* Hanover, N.H.: Office of Instructional Services and Educational Psychology, Dartmouth College, 1975.
   Although somewhat dated, this chapter thoroughly evaluates teaching effectiveness in large classes. A decision chart on p. 55 helps to clarify important goals and necessary procedures for constructive evaluation.

Wales, C. E., and Nardi, A. "What Can You Do to Improve Student Performance in a Large Class?" *Engineering Education,* 1981, *71* (5), 336–340.
   The authors identify four variables that contribute to student success and explain how to increase their positive effect. Contains many good, usable suggestions.

How Faculty in Other Disciplines Cope
with Large Classes

Hudson, H. T. "Teaching Physics to a Large Lecture Section." *The Physics Teacher,* 1985, *23* (2), 80–84.
   Four sensible beginning premises provide the foundation for a well-organized and -managed large class.

Rosenkoetter, J. S. "Teaching Psychology to Large Classes: Videotapes, PSI, and Lecturing." *Teaching Psychology,* 1984, *11* (2), 85–87.

Although based on teaching psychology, the techniques proposed are viable in a number of disciplines. The suggestion regarding use of videotaped demonstration is especially worth consideration.

Silverstein, B. "Teaching a Large Lecture Course in Psychology: Turning Defeat into Victory." *Teaching of Psychology,* 1982, *9* (3), 150–155.

The author writes about general education goals and how they relate to instruction occurring in large-class environments. This author's experience is based on a 1200-student course.

Locating Good General References on Teaching Large Courses

Gleason, M. "An Instructor Survival Kit: For Use with Large Classes." *AAHE Bulletin,* 1986, *39* (2), 10–14.

A collection of ideas and resources are proposed for use with large classes with practical advice and relevant resources.

McGee, R. "Practical Problems of Mass Instruction—A Personal Memorandum," and "Afterword." In R. McGee (ed.), *Teaching the Mass Class.* Washington, D.C.: American Sociological Association, 1986.

This experienced instructor of large classes offers information and advice anyone contemplating mass class instruction should read. Included is particularly good advice on mental and emotional preparation for teaching the class.

McKeachie, W. J. *Teaching Tips: A Guidebook for the Beginning College Teacher.* Lexington, Mass.: Heath, 1986.

Chapters 19–22 (8th ed.) are devoted to various aspects of teaching large classes. Included are some suggestions for modifying the impact of large classes, some alternative instructional strategies, and some good advice on maintaining order in large classes.

Teaching Large Classes. Urbana-Champaign: Office of Instructional and Management Services, University of Illinois, n.d.

Four pages with sound advice for the faculty on planning and implementing the basic instructional activities in a large class.

Maryellen Gleason Weimer is head of the Instructional Development Program at Pennsylvania State University.

Mary-Margaret Kerns is a Ph.D. candidate in the Department of Educational Psychology at Pennsylvania State University.

Index